The Art and Craft of
PAPIER MÂCHÉ

The Art and Craft of
PAPIER MÂCHÉ

Juliet Bawden

Photography by Peter Marshall

MITCHELL BEAZLEY

For Ann Scampton and Ray Moxley

Edited and designed by
Mitchell Beazley International Ltd,
Artists House, 14–15 Manette Street,
London W1V 5LB

Art Editor **Larraine Lacey**
Editor **Linda Seward**
Assistant Editor **Sarah Polden**
Editorial Assistant **Jaspal Kharay**
Production **Ted Timberlake**
Senior Executive Art Editor **Jacqui Small**
Senior Executive Editor **Bob Saxton**

Photography **Peter Marshall**
Illustrations **Kevin Hart**

Reprinted 1990, 1991

**Note: The papier mâché designs shown in this book are the
copyright of the individual artists, and may not be copied for
commercial purposes.**

A CIP catalogue for this book is available from the British Library

ISBN 0 85533 768 0

The publishers have made every effort to ensure that all instructions
given in this book are accurate and safe, but they cannot accept
liability for any resulting injury, damage or loss to either person or
property whether direct or consequential and howsoever arising. The
author and publishers will be grateful for any information which will
assist them in keeping future editions up to date.

Typeset in Bembo by Litho Link Ltd, Welshpool, Powys, Wales
Colour reproduction by Scantrans Pte Ltd, Singapore
Printed in Spain by Graficas Estella, S.A., Navarra

Title pages: A detail of a papier mâché wall plate that mixes collage and calligraphy. (Carolyn Quartermaine)

This page: A detail from Parakeet Singh, a piece inspired by the vibrant colours of India. (Katherine Virgils)

Contents

Foreword

The aim of this book is to inspire and instruct — and to convey something of the excitement of papier mâché as a medium for making a vast range of objects, from pots and picture frames to dolls and carnival masks, all beautifully decorated.

The irresistible appeal of papier mâché lies in a combination of three things — the ease with which it can be made and worked; its immense versatility; and the ready availability of materials. Everything you need to make a picture frame, or a bowl, or a vase, or a piece of jewelry, can be found already in most households. For most people, newspaper and scraps of cardboard packing accumulate anyway — so it is easy to set them aside in a cupboard somewhere to recycle later into fine works of craftsmanship.

In this book I explore just some of the limitless possibilities of papier mâché. The structure of the book is straightforward:

First, I provide some historical background, looking at a few key themes in the development of papier mâché. I also look at folk art aspects — the way in which papier mâché has been used, and still is used, to embody the traditional values, beliefs and mythologies of other cultures.

Then follows a basic primer of techniques, which explains the principal methods of making and decorating papier mâché objects. The techniques I describe here have been evolved by a long process of experiment, and have been found to work well for lots of people. However, they should not be taken as fixed prescriptions.

After dealing with the techniques, I move on to individual categories of work — objects to add distinction to an interior (such as frames, pots and furniture),

fun fashion accessories, dolls and masks, and works of art or pure self-expression. I hope that the pieces illustrated will prove inspirational, but it would be a pity — and very much against the philosophy of this book — if readers attempted to produce slavish copies of what they see here. Again, my aim is to encourage people to make discoveries for themselves. I give step-by-step instructions for specific projects (in many cases based on the method used by a particular papier mâché artist), but you will obtain more pleasure from papier mâché if you work out your own variations.

Lastly, some thankyous. Above all, it is with pleasure that I offer a grateful tribute to the artists who generously contributed work to be photographed for this book. A full list of these contributors is given on page 140. Their pieces show a wide range of styles and ambitions, and displayed together like this, between two covers, make the most telling case possible for the boundless potential of papier mâché.

Thanks are due also to the Mitchell Beazley team, for their enthusiasm and professionalism; to Valerie Wade for loaning some antique papier mâché objects; to Andrea Milburn (Museum of London) and Pauline Cockrill (Bethnal Green Museum of Childhood) for historical information; to Oxfam Trading for information on folk artefacts; and to the Wilson and Gough Gallery, 106 Draycott Ave, London SW3 (agents of Sarah Simpson).

Juliet Bawden

This large-scale abstract sculpture, Curved Flute (84inches/213cm long), was constructed from newspaper and glue layered onto a specially formed wire framework. The piece was then decorated in striking colours. The sculpture reflects the very precise approach of the artist Julia Manheim, who was formerly a jeweller. (Julia Manheim)

The following pages look at some historic aspects of papier mâché — in both the East and the West. In the 19th century the medium was used in Europe and America for trays, boxes and other household objects, decorated with virtuosity. Dolls (page 15) were also widely made.

Perspectives

Papier mâché is a material that lends itself well to the recreation of historic styles — not only historic or ethnic styles of papier mâché itself, but also pottery styles, as illustrated by the bowl shown on these pages. It is apt then to begin this book by putting the subject into some kind of chronological perspective. We can learn from history and adapt past styles and methods to modern uses. Indeed, many papier mâché artists today follow time-honoured recipes as closely as possible, sometimes modifying them to take account of the materials available.

For centuries the production of paper was time-consuming and limited. As a result, paper was quite expensive, and further use of it was sought after it had served its original purpose. This led to the development of the craft of papier mâché. Papier mâché has been used to produce objects in many different cultures all over the world because it is such an easily accessible, inexpensive and flexible medium.

An exact historical definition of this technique is difficult as the origins of the words "papier mâché" are disputed by historians. The common assumption is that the term "papier mâché" is a combination of the French word for "chew," which is *mâcher*, and for paper, *papier*. However, the Oxford English Dictionary holds a different view: "although composed of French words...(the term) appears not to be of French origin." Only in recent years has the phrase been recognized in French dictionaries, and then merely

defined as *papier mouillé*, or "moulded paper."

Shirley Spaulding Devoe, a papier mâché historian, claims that the term papier mâché was used by the French emigré workers in the London papier mâché shops of the 18th century. She backs up her statement with an exchange between Mr Twigg, a fruiterer of Covent Garden, and Mrs Joseph Nollekens, the wife of an 18th-century sculptor:

"Mr Twigg remarked that the house at 27 James Street in London was once a shop used by two old French women who had come to England to chew paper for the manufacture of papier mâché products. 'Ridiculous!' Mrs Nollekens replied, adding that 'the elder Mr Wilton ... was the person who employed people from France to work in the papier mâché factory which he had established in Edward Street, Cavendish Square.' None the less, Mr Twigg insisted that his two women had also chewed paper, buying

The versatility of papier mâché is eloquently demonstrated by this large bowl made from pulped paper. Curved strips of copper were embedded into a covering of gesso (see pages 66-7). The squiggles inside the rim add a historic Grecian feel. Other examples of this artist's work can be seen on pages 59, 64-5 and 67. (Carey Mortimer).

cuttings from stationers and bookbinders and preparing the paper in that way in order to keep the process secret in the days before it was mashed by machines."[1]

Jo Elizabeth Gerken, author of a book on papier mâché dolls, could not find the term papier mâché in the *Description des Arts et Métiers par l'Académie des Sciences* published in 1761. The first mention of papier mâché in a French publication appeared in September 1778 in *The Journal de l'Agriculture du Commerce*, which cited the term from an English source, in a translation from a book of household management, *Handmaid to the Arts*, published in 1758. It referred to papier mâché as French for "mashed paper". Ms Gerken goes on to say that the Elizabethan word "mash" meant to mix with water, and this may in part account for the English pronunciation of the word.[2]

Whether we think of papier mâché as being chewed paper or mashed paper we are in fact talking about the same thing — a substance that owes its distinctive qualities to the presence of paper fibre in its composition.

The Eastern World

The Chinese invented paper at the beginning of the 2nd century AD. The manufacture of both pulped paper and plasterboard followed on from this. The Chinese used papier mâché as a material for making war helmets which were toughened by lacquering. In 1910 Ryuzo Torii discovered the remains of red lacquered pot lids in the shell mounds of Port Arthur in Manchuria's Kwantung Territory. These shards are now thought to be of the Han dynasty, circa AD 206.

In the 8th century there was a war between China and Persia, during which some Chinese craftsmen were captured and sent to Samarkand, which was in Arab hands. The Chinese prisoners taught the Arabs how to make paper from old fish nets, rags and other waste materials; this eventually led to the recycling of waste paper into papier mâché objects. From Samarkand paper-making spread to Morocco via Damascus. Near the end of the 10th century paper had widely replaced papyrus and its

*Left, top: This Indian tray and pen case, produced in Kashmir in the 19th century, reflect a Moslem heritage of craftsmanship. The paintwork and gold leaf would have been applied free-hand. Pen cases were among the earliest objects made from papier mâché in Kashmir, providing the name for the local technique in the 15th century, **Kar-i-qalam** (pen-case work) (see page 18). (Valerie Wade)*

Left, bottom: This pen set, made in Kashmir in the 19th century, comprises a box for papers, a pen, letter-opener and a small pot for extra nibs. The background is lacquered; the realistic, colourful flowers and birds are Italianate. (Valerie Wade)

Far right: Lamp stands were among the more popular imports to the West. This 19th-century Kashmiri example would have been made from pulped paper, pressed into moulds and finished in high-gloss varnish. (Valerie Wade)

production extended northward to Spain, France and Germany. It is thought that the Italians learned to make papier mâché from the Orient via the Venetian trade, and from Italy the art spread to Persia and India.

Persian craftsmen were producing papier mâché plates, mirror cases, pencil boxes, toys and other small objects during the 18th and 19th centuries as a cottage industry. Indians were also producing these items, decorated with designs of small flowers and foliage in a Florentine manner. These designs were probably introduced into Kashmir in the 17th century at the time of the building of the Taj Mahal.

France

From the mid-17th century, French craftsmen showed an interest in papier mâché as a commercially viable medium; they were the first in Europe to do so. The stimulus came from Far Eastern imports that were arriving in the West in ever-increasing quantities: Chinese and Japanese papier mâché, like Chinese porcelain, inspired emulation. Interest in papier mâché spread from France to England in the 1670s.

However, unlike porcelain, papier mâché in the West was slow to take off. Not until the mid-18th century was it employed on a large scale. Papier mâché's heyday in western Europe was 1770-1870. Innovations came from France. The use of papier mâché to imitate stucco and plaster decoration began in France in the middle of the century and was adopted in England within five years or so; papier mâché furniture and objects of virtu also first appeared in France. However, the greatest scale of papier mâché production was in England.

The most typical pieces of French papier mâché are snuffboxes made from the mid-18th century, using the pulping process, decorated in *vernis martin*. This is a generic term for a French lacquering technique that was invented by Guillaume Martin and his brothers, in imitation of Chinese finishes. Many French objects of virtu were made from theatre playbills, which became redundant after each night's performance, and old posters stripped from billboards.

Papier mâché furniture was most popular in France from 1840 to 1880. This is also the golden age of furniture production in England and America. As with other objects in papier mâché, the largest output came from England — and included probably the finest pieces of papier mâché furniture ever made.

Germany

The French exported their papier mâché boxes to Germany in the early 18th century. Frederick the Great is said to have had a snuffbox in every room of his palace! He established a papier mâché factory in 1765 in Berlin. Early German snuffboxes were very popular even though they were of the rudest and simplest type.

George Sigmund Stobwasser was an excellent German craftsman who is known for his flat, round, papier mâché boxes. In 1763, at the age of only twenty-three, he established a factory, under the auspices of the Duke of Brunswick, where he produced snuffboxes and tobacco boxes.

An extraordinary demonstration of the versatility of papier mâché was a watch made in Germany in 1883, constructed entirely of papier mâché and paper. It was the masterpiece of a Dresden watchmaker who claimed that it was durable and performed as well as any metal watch. The timepiece also demonstrates the skill of the craftsman.

Much more typical of German output in the 19th century are papier mâché dolls' heads, produced in great quantities. These could be very sophisticated, detailed and tough (see page 15).

Russia

The manufacture of papier mâché was started in Russia in 1830 in an attempt to imitate Continental and English papier mâché ware. The basic material consisted of layered paper which was softened by heat and shaped on wooden moulds and then saturated three times with flax-seed oil. The articles were then primed with a mixture of native red clay, Holland soot and oil, and were subsequently dried, lacquered and, finally, polished.

Lacquering on papier mâché in Russia was first done in Fedoskino near Moscow by peasant craftsmen who were pioneers in the painting of folk art on papier

mâché. Between 1825 and 1830 a large factory was set up and run by the Lukutin family. The Lukutins became the first and foremost producers of snuffboxes, cigarette cases, chests of various kinds, tea trays and many other useful articles.

England

In the 17th and 18th centuries there was a great deal of interest in papier mâché lacquerware in England, and instructions on the making of papier mâché were published in many books and magazines. Until the last quarter of the 18th century, production was mainly of architectural and decorative ornaments such as small gilded wall brackets, sconces and small boxes. However, from about 1740 many papier mâché factories, especially in Birmingham and Wolverhampton, in the Midlands, were established for the purpose of producing lacquer or "Japan" ware — a type of papier mâché ware, Oriental in design, which is hard and will take on a high polish after painting.

Japan ware In a catalogue to an exhibition of japanned wares, Yvonne Jones talks about the revival of interest in chinoiseries (a Western imitation of Chinese art) which lasted in varying degrees from the 1770s through to the 1820s. This interest coincided with inventor Henry Clay's patent of a papier mâché process in 1772. Clay devised a method of gluing together sheets of specially prepared paper under heat to form strong heat-resistant panels, originally known as paper ware, then later as papier mâché. "This improved, heat-resistant material was capable of being japanned without fear of warping or cracking and enabled objects formerly made from wood or metal to be made from paper."[3] All sorts of objects began to be made by this method, such as highly varnished panels or roofs for coaches, wheel carriages and sedan chairs, panels for rooms, doors and cabins of ships, cabinets, bookcases, screens, chimney pieces, tables and tea trays.[4] The vogue for amateur japanning developed as a result of the interest in things Chinese and Henry Clay's marvellous papier mâché methods.

Edmund Verney, writing in the 1760s to his eight-year-old daughter, reveals how quickly japanning became an admired accomplishment for young ladies. Molly Verney attended "Mrs Priest's School at Chelsey" where the art of japanning boxes was taught. Her father wrote, "I find you have a desire to learn to japan, as you call it, and I approve of it; so I shall of anything that is Good and Virtuous … tho' they come from Japan and never so farr and looke of Indian Hue and Colour, for I admire all accomplishments that will render you considerable and Lovely in the sight of God and Man."[5]

Dictionaries of arts and sciences in which the japanning process was fully described became widely available. In 1758 Robert Sayer published a volume of charming engravings by Jean Baptiste Pillement and other artists, suitable for ornamenting various objects.

Architectural papier mâché Although the manufacture of papier mâché ornament for architectural purposes, as opposed to papier mâché for the japanning industry, was of some importance in the 18th century, it wasn't until the 19th century that it was greatly increased. Two companies, both from London, led the field: Jackson and Son, and Charles Frederick Bielefeld.

The Jackson firm was founded by George Jackson who was a carver of wooden moulds for Robert Adam in 1765. This firm made mouldings and other architectural embellishments of carton-pierre, composition and papier mâché.

Charles Bielefeld, an inventor and manufacturer, introduced papier mâché panels that measured 6 x 8 feet/1.8 x 2.5 metres and were ½ inch (13mm) in thickness; he received his patent for this in 1846. The panels were moulded on a skeleton support of wood and were tough and soundproof, and said to be more durable for painting than canvas was. They were used for bulkheads and cabin partitions in some of the steamers of the day and in railway carriages shown in the Great Exhibition of 1851, in London.

However, Bielefeld's most interesting product was a village of ten prefabricated houses. The houses were commissioned by a man named Mr Seymour who was planning to emigrate to Australia and establish a village there. When the village was temporarily set up on the factory grounds, heavy rains caused flooding, and the houses stood in two feet/60cm of water without drainage. The fate of the village is unknown, but it is thought that some of the houses may have survived a long time. Certainly, a papier mâché church erected near Bergen in Norway in 1793 lasted thirty-seven years before being demolished.

The architectural and decorative ornaments made during this period, such as small wall brackets, sconces, small boxes, moulded ceiling ornaments, mirror frames and girandoles, were frequently gilded but not japanned. They were made from pulp, which because of its lightness was suitable even for ceiling ornaments but which, being brittle, was unsuitable for japanning, except on the smallest items such as snuffboxes.

The manufacture of architectural papier mâché was based on a number of "shops" where different processes were carried out. The dipping shop contained wide, shallow vats of linseed oil and tar spirit into which large sheets of blank paper would be dipped for protection from beetles and other pests. There were also large copper pots in which paper paste was made from flour and glue boiled in water.

The next process was the moulding and pasting. This work was carried out by women and girls. The paper, which came in sheets measuring 3 x 4 feet/ 91 x 122cm, was first cut to shape and then covered with paste on both sides. The paper was then placed on a greased mould and worked over with a flat trowel-like tool to remove bubbles and other irregularities. The edge was then shaped by hand. Two or more additional sheets were pasted on one side only and then added to the piece in the mould. The article was then stove-dried at 100°-120°F/38°-49°C. When the object was dry it was filed smooth and then three more layers were pasted and added to the mould. The process was repeated until the piece was made of the required thickness, which could be anything between 10 and 120 sheets, depending on the treatment and final use to which the piece was to be put.

Once the article was thoroughly dry it was saturated in linseed oil and stoved for about a day and a half at 200°-260°F/93°-127°C. Oiling and stoving made the product hard, strong and water-resistant; they also turned the paper from grey to brown.

The common, as opposed to the best, method of making papier mâché was to pulp the paper by reducing it to a clay-like consistency and compressing it in moulds with a hydraulic screw. After the objects had been shaped, they would then be decorated.

Decoration Early decoration of English-made papier mâché was usually of an all-over floral design. By the beginning of the 19th century the central panels on boxes, trays and the like were often left clear and only the outer edges and borders would be decorated. During the 120 years of papier mâché manufacture in England, the most usual background colour was black. However red, yellow, green and blue were sometimes used.

Until the 1820s, enamel in bronze, and silver or gold in leaf or powder form, were used for decoration. The effect of the powder was filmy, whereas the metal leaf produced solid lines. In 1825 Jennens and Bettridge, a well-known Midlands firm who manufactured papier mâché, introduced mother-of-pearl inlay as a means of decoration. The late 18th century saw a Gothic revival which was reflected in the decoration of papier mâché objects of the day. England was also importing Chinese lacquer, so the papier mâché manufacturers started to produce their own Chinese-style lacquer (Japan ware) to compete with the highly popular imports.

Flowers were popular as motifs for decoration. James Grimes reproduced hawthorn blossom and snowdrops. William Jackson painted lily of the valley and David Sargent ferns. After 1850, marbling, as well as graining in imitation of such woods as walnut, maple, and rosewood, became popular.

As the designs became more intricate and fine, other novelties were sought within the industry. But papier mâché by this time had become overexposed. The market steadily declined, and in order to remain commercially viable makers allowed their products to degenerate towards the cheap and shoddy. The final nail in the coffin was the introduction of electroplating in the 1850s. Electroplaters could produce trays, for example, far more quickly and less expensively than japanners and yet their products appealed to the same customers. The last papier mâché manufacturer to close in England was McCallum and Hodson in 1920.

America

It is well known that papier mâché goods were exported to America by Jennens and Bettridge of Birmingham, England, and probably by other Birmingham factories. George Washington was interested in acquiring papier mâché for the ceilings of two rooms at Mount Vernon and sent an order to his London factor.

In 1850 the Litchfield Manufacturing Company set up a factory on the banks of the Bantam River in Litchfield, Connecticut. It occupied four or five buildings, the largest of which was three floors high, measuring 50 × 80 feet/15 × 24 metres. Between 50 and 80 men and women were employed. The directors of the company brought japanners from Wolverhampton and Oxfordshire in England to direct the work and teach the locals in the art of japanning and painting. Experienced Wolverhampton workers could earn between six and ten dollars a day and work in clean and pleasant surroundings in the new factory.

At home they earned much less (30 to 60 shillings) for a 66-hour week. They manufactured letter holders, card trays, standing screens and yarn holders. In 1851 the company started concentrating on clock cases which were made of fairly thick pasteboard, japanned in black and ornamented with paint, gold and mother-of-pearl. Clock making was a big industry in Connnecticut, and the Litchfield company was the only maker of papier mâché clock cases. Each case bore a paper label printed by the press of the *Litchfield Republican* newspaper. It is said that the Litchfield varnish was faulty and that it shows a bubbled surface, due to lack of polishing. However, the goods have a freshness and originality all of their own. In 1851 the *Litchfield Republican* enthused: "We cannot speak too highly of the English and German artists who principally do the ornamented part of the work."

One of Litchfield's most favoured forms of design was a single rose of inlaid pearl-shell, with gilt leaves and stems. This is very interesting, because at the time the only company allowed to use shell decoration was Jennens and Bettridge, who had taken out a patent in 1825 to protect its use. In the light of this evidence, it is thought that some of the emigrant workers at Litchfield must have previously worked for Jennens and Bettridge in England. In 1854, the Litchfield Manufacturing Company exhibited some of their papier mâché clocks at the New York World's Fair: these were described as "the best display of goods in the whole exhibit".

It was also in that year that P.T. Barnum, a stockholder in the company, persuaded the other stockholders to move to East Bridgeport, Connecticut, and to merge with The Terry Clock Company, which then became The Terry and Barnum Manufacturing Company. The following summer, in 1855, the company merged again with the Jerome Clock Company. At this date papier mâché manufacuring came to an end in Litchfield.

Another Connecticut papier mâché factory was the Wadhams Manufacturing Company, started in 1851 and closed in 1863. The company produced a range of items, including desks, stair rods, sewing work boxes and even chess boards.

Daniel Cooksley, the owner of the Bird Japanning Company of Boston, learned his trade in the place of his birth, Birmingham in England. He employed five people, and among other things made papier mâché buttons which he japanned and then gave away to friends.

At the end of the 19th century an Act of Congress made it possible to macerate retired bank notes. The resulting pulp was mixed with a solution of soda, ash and lime which destroyed the identity of the bank notes. This pulpy mixture was then moulded into busts of prominent Americans and replicas of national monuments, which were sold to the public. These souvenirs stood about 4 inches/10cm high. They were not decorated in any way, the mottled grey colour of the pulp providing ornament enough.

Dolls

In France, papier mâché was used for dolls' heads as early as the 16th century. From around 1810 the toy factories at Sonneberg in Thüringia, Germany, started to mass-produce heads using a pressure process that superseded hand kneading. The dollmakers of the Nürnberg area were the first to utilize waste from paper mills. Papier mâché dolls remained in vogue until the 1870s, and are now highly collectable.

The first dolls were made in moulds that had wooden cores down their middles. As dollmaking developed, the recipe was refined and more ingredients added. The proportions of pulp to other materials, and the nature of those materials, varied from country to country.

The main materials used to make dolls' heads were pulp, filler and binder. The pulp consisted of raw, shredded, beaten or mashed paper, either in dry fibrous form or moistened with water. Although, to qualify as papier mâché, it was felt that the pulp should be made of wood or paper fibres, in fact it often comprised a variety of different fibres, rags being the most usual. Samuel Hooper took out a patent in 1790 to make various articles from leather parings. In 1883 a British patent was granted to Johnson and Maloney to use broccoli, cabbage and cauliflower.

The fillers were indigenous, easily accessible materials. Thus in India, the filler was rice flour. In Germany rye meal was often used, to produce an early type of papier mâché known as *Brotteig* (literally, "bread dough"), employed to form dolls free-hand as well as in moulds. In the north of England in the 19th century, mashed potato was favoured! Italian and English dolls incorporated clay and sand as fillers. By the end of the 19th century, ground chalk, also known as whiting, was used by many doll makers.

The binder was usually glue-water, although honey-water and sometimes gum arabic were used in some areas. Glue-water was made by boiling dried animal glue in water until a thick, syrupy consistency resulted. The British used isinglass, a pure form of gelatin, to bind some of their dolls.

Occasionally old recipes for papier mâché mention other ingredients. Resin was used to give a hard smooth surface. Potash was added either to neutralize the acidity of the dough or to act as a deterrent against insects and rodents. German dollmakers sometimes added tobacco leaves to the dough mix. Kolioquinte, a bitter gourd-like vine fruit with an extreme purging action, features in some recipes; it is also known as bitter cucumber. Garlic, either alone or combined with vermouth, was also used as an insect repellant. The smells left by the glue were often unpleasant, so some recipes called for the addition of deodorizers such as cinnamon or cloves.

In America one of the most important dollmakers was Ludwig Greiner of Philadelphia, whose dolls had papier mâché heads (patented 1858) lined with linen or muslin.

"Composition" dolls are related to true papier mâché but tend to be harder, as they were often made with more filler and less pulp. There was also an inferior grey cardboard-like material known as "carton", which had a high proportion of pulp in relation to binder and filler (indeed, sometimes there was no filler at all); it was popular in the 1920s and 30s.

Papier mâché products made in traditional rural styles can offer a rich source of inspiration for craftworkers today. Their appeal derives from the marriage of bright colours, inventive patterns and deep symbolic associations.

Folk

ART TRADITIONS

The craft of papier mâché has been, and still is, carried out in many rural communities, often following traditional styles that have not changed for centuries. The Indian region of Kashmir, for example, has a tradition of making folk art papier mâché, as does Mexico. The Japanese make dolls from the material and the Philippinos make large animals. Craftsmen in Spain and Italy produce papier mâché puppets.

As papier mâché is such an inexpensive material, large numbers of giant-sized masks and heads and parts of costumes can be produced at low cost for use at carnival, fiesta or festival time.

Japan

In Japan, toys and dolls are made in one or a combination of the following materials: wood, clay, paper (including papier mâché) and straw. These take the form of lions, oxen, foxes and small bells, often made as propitiatory gifts to ensure divine protection for agriculture. Toys made as replicas of birds, dogs, tigers and monkeys are considered to have powers against evil spirits, although some are also made just for play. Papier mâché toys have been the traditional playthings of the upper classes of the Okinawa Islands (SW Japan) for generations. It is felt by many that the high quality of the work produced reflects the strong religious sense that prevails there.[6]

It was during the Edo period, from the beginning of the 17th century, when peace followed an era of wars, that folk toys first gained their wide public appeal. Many adults would take home gifts to the children after worshipping at the *miya*, or shrine, and these gifts eventually took the form of toys. Thus, having started out as ritual objects with powers of exorcism, folk toys in Japan have come to be considered gifts from the gods to protect children.

Some of the toys represent folk heros and have myths attached to them. Many of the stories are associated with the sea. One such story is about Kinko, a Chinese recluse who lived in Japan. He painted pictures of fish and lived for two hundred years. One day he was asked by the king of the fish if he would like to be taken through the river world for a short trip. After a month he returned on the back of a carp. This event was witnessed by 10,000 disciples who were purifying themselves in the river. Kinko begged them not to kill any more fish. Then he dived back in the river and was gone for good.

The sea bream, a red-skinned saltwater fish found in abundance along the coast of Japan, is called the "king of fishes" by the Japanese. It is a highly prized delicacy and is associated with daily food and with Ebisu, the god of plenty; it is an emblem of good fortune. The sea bream is sometimes made as a pull-along fish on wheels or as a lantern. Sea bream lanterns date from the end of the 19th century when they were used as decorations in summer festivals.

The badger is also a very popular image in Japan, and is well known for its mischievous pranks

As well as their obvious association with wildfowling, ducks have symbolic meanings in various cultures: for example, in China they are emblems of marital fidelity. These examples, from India, show how papier mâché, smoothed, sanded and varnished, can work effectively as a substitute for carved wood. The highly controlled, tight design, with accurate duck beaks, eyes and feathers all painted in fine detail, adds to the illusion. (General Trading Company)

which are generally humorous and frequently bungled. He is supposed to take on all sorts of disguises and deceive or annoy wayfarers. Badger dolls are most popular in the Shikoku and Chugoko districts where these animals abound.

The beckoning cat, another popular image in Japan, can be found in a variety of materials, including papier mâché. The story behind the image concerns a cat who helped her distressed master by earning money for him. The cat became a symbol of money-earning potential, or *Fukumaneki*, which in translation means "fortune beckoning".

India

Papier mâché has been made in the Kashmir region of India since the 15th century. It was originally known in Kashmir as *Kar-i-qalam* (pen-case works). At this time it was confined to the ornamentation of cases in which pens were kept. From these beginnings it developed into *Kar-i-munaqqash* used for ornamenting smooth surfaces made of paper pulp or layers of polished paper. As the craft developed, items such as dressing-table ware, bangles, lampshades, cups, bowls, vases, boxes, wall plaques and panels for ceilings were produced.

Today, papier mâché is produced by members of the Moslem community. There are two sects involved in this craft: the Shiaz and the Sunnies. The Shiaz are traditional papier mâché workers, who have passed on the skill from father to son. The Sunnies have no direct tradition and produce work that is considered inferior. Although officially it is understood that papier mâché is done entirely by men, in reality women are often involved in the unskilled drudgery of smoothing the paper pulp in the mould.

India's traditional method of making papier mâché is extremely labour-intensive, and today tends to be used to make curved shapes such as vases. First, waste paper from printing presses is brought in and left to soak in a vat of water for between five and six days. It is then trampled by foot to mix it up, and the water is drained out. The paper is then formed into a pulp by hand. The pulp is placed in moulds for two to three days; each mould forms half of a vase or other object. The hardened pulp is removed from the moulds and the two parts are then joined. The surface is rubbed with a fine local stone to make it smooth and a varnish is applied to make the surface impermeable. The object is painted black, then painted in a pattern in oil. Finally, the object is lacquered to seal and finish it.

India's modern-day method for producing small boxes and containers is a quicker process which involves using strawboard — a kind of rough cardboard, which comes in sheets and is cut with a guillotine or hacksaw to form the basis of the box. Soaked waste paper is then wrapped around the strawboard, building up the layers until the appearance of the object is similar to that achieved by pulping. The parts are then glued together and left to dry. The box is then finished by the traditional method.

The price differential between the strawboard and waste paper methods is minimal because the materials are intrinsically the same, but in terms of labour the methods vary greatly. However, the purchaser will usually be unable to distinguish between the two manufacturing processes.

Patterns are painted on completely freehand: no design guide or stencil is used. The designs are done by all the family, and are freely copied from one family to another.

Mexico

In Mexico, as in Japan, many of the toys and dolls made from papier mâché are tied in with religion and superstition. For example, little Judases are made to commemorate Holy Week.

A favourite toy of the Christmas season is the colourful *piñata*, enjoyed by Mexican children in cities and villages alike. *Piñata*s, fashioned into many different shapes including ships, fish, flowers and stars, are modelled out of papier mâché and hold clay pots packed with sweets, fruit, nuts and small toys. The *piñata* is suspended from a branch of a tree or from a ceiling on a string above the heads of the children. One by one the children are blindfolded and with a stick lash out at the object. Sometimes a parent will join in, adding to the excitement by raising and lowering the rope that is holding the *piñata*. Eventually a crash is heard as the thing breaks, and the children dive forward to collect its treasures.

The Mexicans treat death with humour. The practice of representing death as a skeleton in artistic compositions began with the folk painter Posada. On All Souls' Day, the Mexican Day of the Dead, brightly coloured and decorated skeletons and skulls made from papier mâché are seen all over Mexico City. One can find cardboard coffins from which a skeleton can be made to jump by pulling a string. Sometimes the skeleton figures represent strolling guitar players, *mariachi* bands, or even newspaper delivery boys.

Masks have been traditional in Mexico since before the Spanish conquest. Priests would wear masks representing the faces of the deities they wished to honour. Hunters donned masks bearing the faces of the animals they hoped to kill. Some of these masks were made in rich materials and embellished with mother-of-pearl and turquoise. Masks today are usually made of paper or papier mâché and can be purchased for a few cents. Present-day natives wear masks for the same reasons as their ancestors — to exert magic and to achieve a facial expression for which they feel their own features are inadequate.

Europe

In many small towns all over Europe, puppet shows have been performed periodically by travelling artists. The most famous — and influential — puppet character was Pulcinella, a figure from the Italian Commedia dell'arte tradition who first appeared as a glove puppet in the early 17th century. By way of itinerant Italian puppeteers, Pulcinella spawned hook-nosed, hunchback characters throughout Europe. Variants include Polichinelle in France, Petrushka in Russia and Punch in England. Apart from the last (angry Mr Punch still battles his way through Punch and Judy shows today) the offspring of Pulcinella, and their repertories, continued to develop. By the end of the 18th century the descendants included Guignol in France, Kasperl in Germany, Jan Klaassen in the

Netherlands and Christovita in Spain. All of these characters are national types. Local figures also appeared — for example, the Spanish provinces saw Don Cristobel in Castile, Christofal and Tofol in Catalonia, Tirsitis in Alicante, Teresetes in the Balearic Islands, Tia Norica in Andalusia and Barriga Verde in Galicia. The puppets were traditionally carved in wood for the professionals, while amateur versions were made in papier mâché. However, as plastic took over from wood, the individuality of the puppets was lost, but in reaction to this there has been a return to handmade puppets, this time mainly in papier mâché.

Monstrous giant figures and immense heads known as *cabezudos* are colourful items of medieval origin, made out of papier mâché. They are used during the processions of Corpus Christi Day in southern European towns. The figures may be up to two or three times taller than the person they cover; although they are similar to each other in size, the imagery varies from region to region. They can represent knights, ladies, peasants, kings or queens, and they always appear in pairs, a man and a woman. In 19th-century Barcelona and Valencia, the female figure gave a preview of the next year's fashions. The giants' retinue is formed by young volunteers wearing the immense *cabezudos*, which symbolize the common folk. Their expressions are caricaturish and crude, performing a grotesque pantomime around the giants. The great heads are made of cardboard and papier mâché, but from the waist down they are usually constructed of basketry or light wood.

Top: This hen, a folk artefact from India, has been made by a semi-industrial process. The image is simple, strong, primitive, with very little colour, the feathers, wings, comb markings and beak all painted in quite crude brushstrokes in a soft brown colour. (General Trading Company)

Middle: Fishes are a common papier mâché folk art form in coastal or island communities. This fish-shaped box is from India. (General Trading Company)

Bottom: Cats have magical or good-luck associations in some cultures. This one, with a matt varnish, is from the Philippine Islands. (loaned by Mr and Mrs Frankl Bertram)

TECHNIQUES

One reason for the popularity of papier mâché is that the basic equipment and materials are inexpensive and readily available. The craft can be practised anywhere, without having to purchase special tools.

Before YOU BEGIN

Pages 20-21: These small bowls were constructed over existing moulds (also bowls) using just three or four layers of handmade paper and glue. Strong colour dyes were then painted on. The dyes bled into the paper, softening the strong brushmarks. The result is an unusual combination of bold colour with subtle tones and textures. (Sarah Simpson)

Opposite: A deliberately random form can be attractive, especially if combined with simple but striking decoration, as in this vessel which was water-gilded over a base of gesso to which a layer of bole was applied. (Caroline Gibbs)

Although papier mâché work need not necessarily involve mess, it does require organization and discipline. It is vital to have somewhere that has warm air circulating to store work in progress and facilitate drying. It is essential to thoroughly dry your work or the end-result will be disappointing — distorted in shape and possibly marred by fungus.

If a workroom is not available, a little ingenuity will help, even in cramped work spaces. Inflated balloons that have been used as a basis for making pots (see pages 40-41) can be suspended on pieces of cotton thread and hung from a window sill or doorway or underneath a table. A boiler room or an airing cupboard are good places for drying work. If you are really short of space, consider using the top of warm kitchen cupboards/cabinets.

You will need a source of water, both for mixing paste and for cleaning your equipment. A stove is necessary if you are going to make pulp. You will also need a large flat surface on which to work. A table covered in either a plastic-faced cloth or plenty of old newspaper will do.

There are three basic ways of working with papier mâché: you can use a mould or template (see pages 48-51); you can apply papier mâché to an existing object (pages 32-3 and 36-7); or you can make an armature and cover it with papier mâché (pages 44-5). The papier mâché itself can be made by pulping (pages 26-7) or by layering (pages 34-7).

Basic equipment and materials

Either method:
Large work surface
Newspaper or any other type of paper you wish to use
Paste
Moulds (eg bowls, vases, balloons) or armatures (eg chicken wire, cardboard, wood)
Releasing agent (for use with moulds) — petroleum jelly, talcum powder or clear plastic wrap/saran wrap
Paste or glue
Running water — for mixing paste and washing equipment
Bowls — for mixing paste
Large screw-top jars — for storing paste once it has been made
Fan-assisted oven for drying objects (optional)

Scissors and craft knife — for trimming edges and occasionally cutting paper
Masking tape, brown gummed tape, clear adhesive tape
Tin snips/wire cutters and flat-nosed pliers — if using wire
Fabric, tissue, beads, string, buttons — for surface decoration
Sealers
Paints
Thin rubber gloves (optional)

Layer method only:
Wide brush

Pulp method only:
Large cooking pot
Heat source
Plastic bucket
Sieve
Whisk
Rolling pin
Sandpaper

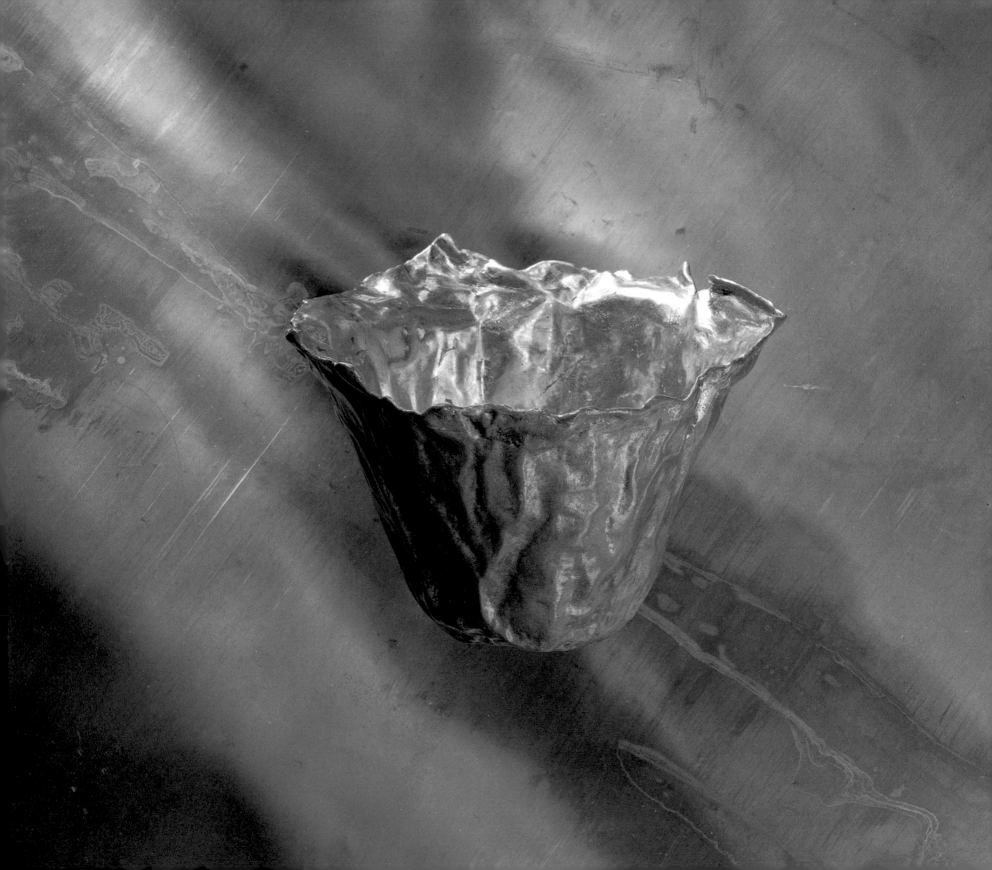

Papers, glues and finishes

Paper

Newsprint tends to be the most popular paper, as it is inexpensive and readily available. However, newspaper can vary in quality and strength. Avoid any that is too heavily printed with a great deal of bold type as this can come off in the wetting process and may affect the glue, making the final object difficult to prime and decorate. Papers with long fibres, such as blotting paper, are excellent for constructions that need to be strong, or for covering a large surface area. Heavier

Wallpaper paste Wallpaper paste (wheat paste) can be obtained in all good hardware stores. Mix it according to the manufacturer's instructions, bearing in mind that a small packet will go a very long way. Keep this mixed paste in an air-tight container to extend its life. NOTE: Many wallpaper pastes contain a fungicide which prevents mould from forming as the papier mâché is drying out.

Polyvinyl acetate (PVA) adhesive, or white glue This is an extremely versatile glue. It can be

papers such as brown wrapping paper and cartridge paper are also good for large pieces of work. Fine papers such as tissue, paper towels and crepe paper are ideal for creasing and for adding fine features.

Paste and glue

The choice of paste or glue depends on the object being made and the purpose to which it is being put: paste takes longer to dry and produces a softer product, while glue is better than paste for fastening paper to wood or metal, and for attaching details at the end of a construction.

Flour and water paste In a saucepan, mix ¼ cup of flour into 1 cup of water. When the mixture is thin, runny and free from lumps, add 5 cups of water that has just been boiled. Gently boil the mixture, stirring constantly, for 2 to 3 minutes, until the mixture thickens. Allow it to cool slightly before using.

used at full strength to produce a tough surface which dries rapidly. For most work you should dilute 3 parts PVA to 1 part water. This makes an excellent sealer and filler and provides a good surface to paint on.

Epoxy This is a very strong adhesive but hard to use in papier mâché work because it is difficult to spread, and needs to be handled with caution as it can be harmful to the skin and eyes. It can be used as a final coating in place of varnish as it produces a hard glossy surface which is almost impervious to liquids.

Vegetable glue This is the most suitable glue for adding fabric or trims to finished pieces — for example, when lining a box with fabric.

Filler

Filler adds bulk to the pulp. You can use either a cellulose filler/spackle, available from DIY stores, or whiting/ground chalk. You can also use a simple ground or powdery substance such as sawdust.

Sealing or priming

You must prime a papier mâché article before painting it. This will prevent the paint from being absorbed by the porous paper, and will also help to stop newsprint bleeding through the paint onto the final design. Before sealing, make sure that the sealer is compatible with the paint or finish which is to be used for decoration. If you are planning to use a water-based paint, seal the papier mâché object with decorator's emulsion

These three papier mâché wall plates have been constructed from silk, layered paper and glue using tissue paper and calligraphy for decoration. The pieces were inspired by the propaganda of the French Revolution. On the top and middle plates the newspaper used in construction has become part of the decoration, as it is visible through the thin sheets of tissue paper. (Carolyn Quartermaine)

paint; paint on the first coat, leave it to dry for 24 hours, then apply a second coat.

Gesso

Gesso is calcium, in the form of ground chalk or gypsum, mixed with an animal glue to produce a white, plastic material. This is painted onto a papier mâché object prior to decoration. When dry, gesso is as hard as stone and can be sanded to a smooth finish. You can make gesso yourself (see the recipe on pages 66-7) or it can be purchased in powder or liquid form. It is best used on heavier papers.

Protecting and waterproofing

To extend the life of your papier mâché objects, there are various treatments that will make them hard, waterproof and fireproof.

Linseed oil When the papier mâché object is completely dry, brush 3 or 4 coats of linseed oil over the entire surface. Bake the object at a temperature of not more than 250°F/120°C until it is completely dry and hard. This will make the object waterproof.

Varnish Varnish dries very slowly and results in a hard finish. It is available in clear, gloss, high gloss, matt or semi-matt, and may be tinted. Give the papier mâché several coats, allowing each coat to dry thoroughly before painting on the next. This will protect and waterproof the papier mâché.

Lacquer This finish can be bought clear or with pigments added. It dries quickly to a hard surface which will protect the papier mâché.

Fireproofing When making a lampshade, candlestick or anything which is going to be used near a heat source, it is advisable to paint the object with fire-retardant. This can be obtained from theatrical prop suppliers and some hardware stores.

Pulping is the process of mixing torn pieces of paper with water and boiling the mixture to a pulp to which an adhesive is added. The end-result is a clay-like substance which may be sculpted or moulded. When untreated, pulped paper tends to produce a coarse finish; this can easily be sanded down.

The pulp method of making papier mâché objects, although it involves a little more preparation work than the layering method, has some major advantages. Because there is only one main stage in the production procedure, the object needs drying only once. Pulp is slightly more substantial than layered papier mâché, especially if a filler has been added; the filler can be plain, for example chalk or cellulose filler/spackle, or can have an interesting texture of its own, such as sawdust. Pulping is ideal for large items where stability is all-important.

Pulp lends itself well to surface decoration. When wet, it is very pliable, which means that intricate work is possible. Moist pulp is an ideal base for impressed designs. Dry pulp may be carved, filled or smoothed to a fine finish.

You can make pulp from a variety of papers including newspaper, sugar paper, tissue paper, corrugated paper, egg boxes and computer printout paper. Newspaper will produce a coarse pulp. Thin paper, such as tissue, will produce a fine pulp that results in a porcelain-like finish.

How to make pulp

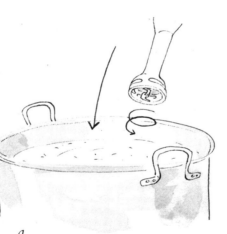

a

b

Equipment and materials

Heat source (cooker ring/burner)
Sink and running water
Plastic bucket
Large wooden spoon
Large cooking pot — a large jam-making pancheon/saucepan is ideal
Metal egg whisk, hand-held electric whisk or blender
Fine mesh sieve or a

jam-maker's straining bag
Plastic mixing bowl
4 double-page sheets (16 pages) of newspaper
2 tablespoons of whiting/ground chalk (or cellulose filler/spackle)
2 tablespoons of white glue
1 tablespoon of linseed oil (either baked or raw)
2 drops oil of wintergreen or oil of cloves
2 tablespoons of wallpaper (wheat) paste

The following recipe is taken from Papier Mâché Artistry by Dona Z. Meilach[7]. It will make 1 quart (approximately 1 litre) of pulp:

1 Tear the paper into pieces no larger than 1 inch/2.5cm square, tearing in the direction of the grain. Put the paper into the bucket, cover with water and allow the mixture to soak overnight.

2 Next day, transfer the soaked paper into a large cooking pot and boil for 20 minutes in 2 quarts (2 litres) of water to loosen the fibres. Use the whisk or

blender to transform the paper into a pulp (a).

3 Strain the paper pulp in the sieve or straining bag, tapping and shaking out the surplus water (b).

4 After the pulp has been strained it will form a soft wet lump which can be held in the hand. This will consist of 90 percent water. Compress the pulp between your two hands to force more water out, but do not squeeze too hard or the pulp will become tough and unworkable (c).

5 Put the soft wet pulp into the mixing bowl. Add the two heaped tablespoons of whiting/ground chalk, two

To make pulped paper you will need paper, water and paste (or glue). If using a flour and water paste you will need to add a proprietary fungicide. (For more on paste and paper, see pages 24-5.)

The quantities mentioned in the recipe that follows can be varied considerably. More filler makes a whiter, denser pulp. More paste or glue gives a stronger finish. If you find the mixture is too watery, add more wallpaper (wheat) paste.

The paste and glue serve as binders. The whiting/ground chalk (or cellulose filler/spackle) acts as a filler; it also improves the colour of the finished product and adds density. Linseed oil makes the pulp easier to work with and provides added toughness. Oil

of cloves and wintergreen prevent the pulp from going sour. This can happen quite quickly if the pulp is untreated, and is a waste of materials, time and effort.

An easier approach altogether is to use instant pulp, which can be purchased from craft shops.

Store any unused pulp in a plastic bag in the refrigerator. Store larger quantities in a plastic dustbin/garbage can with a lid.

Large pieces of pulp must have warm air circulating around them in order to dry in a cool climate. A fan-assisted oven, set on a low temperature, is useful for drying small objects. Or, you could leave your piece of work to dry in a boiler room or an airing cupboard. Be patient; pulp dries slowly.

tablespoons of white glue and one tablespoon of linseed oil. Then add a few drops of oil of wintergreen and mix the ingredients together with a large spoon (d).

6 *When the pulp has been thoroughly mixed, sprinkle in two spoonfuls of dry wallpaper (wheat) paste; stir again. The mixture is now ready to use.*

The earrings here are made from pulp built up over simple cardboard cutouts. The bangle consists of a cardboard base to which pulped paper has been added.

Each piece of jewelry has been painted with bright abstract patterns, the glitter of the gold paint wittily mimicking the sparkle of real jewels. (Louise Vergette)

The illustrations here show three useful moulds:
Bowl: the easiest shape to work with.
Vase: in order to remove the mould, papier mâché applied to the outside would have to be cut in half and rejoined.
Jelly mould: these can be plastic or lightweight metal.

Papier mâché may be applied onto an existing object or mould which is removed once the papier mâché casting is dry. The cast papier mâché has the same shape as the mould, and you have re-created that shape without permanently covering or destroying the original. The advantage of working with moulds in this way is that they can be used over and over again to make many copies.

A gently curving bowl is the best mould for a beginner to use, because it is easy to remove the dried papier mâché from it. However, you can use even a waisted vase shape as a mould. This is done simply by

cutting the papier mâché in half once it is dry, removing the original mould, then using pulp or strips of paper and glue to rejoin the two pieces.

Working over existing moulds enables you to create an endless variety of papier mâché objects. The shape of the objects cast from a mould will all be roughly the same, allowing for variations of texture and thickness; absolute consistency will ultimately depend upon the craftsman. The individuality of pieces made in a mould derives from the ways in which they are finished and decorated — and the ornamental possibilities are endless.

Choosing and using a mould

These assorted containers (opposite) are made from handmade paper and glue layered over existing moulds — a vase, a glass tumbler and a bowl. As shown by these pieces, moulds do not require a thick application of papier mâché; this artist uses as few as two layers of paper on moulds. The paper was dyed before

construction and the edges left purposefully raw and rough. The combination and layering of contrasting colours and shapes of paper produces a decorative, three-dimensional collage effect. The pieces were finally varnished inside and outside for protection.(Maureen Hamilton-Hill)

When using a mould, bear in mind the following guidelines:

1 *Always apply a releasing agent to a mould so that the papier mâché won't stick to the mould when you are trying to remove it. You can use petroleum jelly, talcum powder, oil, clear plastic wrap/saran wrap or strips of plain wet newspaper (without glue) for the first coat.*

2 *Be sure to cover the edges of the mould with the releasing agent: unless you do this the papier mâché will be more difficult to remove.*

3 *When the papier mâché is thoroughly dry, firmly grasp the edges of the mâché on opposite sides of the mould and twist gently.*

4 *If the papier mâché does not come out easily, a vacuum may have built up between the two surfaces; if this is the case, pierce the papier mâché with a pin in several spots, then try twisting again.*

5 *If you have used an oddly shaped mould, remove the dried papier mâché from the mould by cutting it evenly in half, starting at the top and cutting around.*

6 *Join the two pieces together by applying additional pulp or layers of paper and glue.*

7 *Seal, finish and decorate the papier mâché object using one of the methods described on pages 52-67.*

Surprising results can be achieved by applying pulped paper to "found" moulds. A wide range of objects you use — and perhaps overlook — in daily life will serve as moulds. Even a simple bowl offers countless possibilities.

Pulp

OVER A MOULD

A mould may be used over and over again to create a series of identical shapes. Look around your house for suitable objects: baskets, dishes, bowls, saucepans, toys — the scope is virtually endless. Margarine tubs and plastic bowls are excellent as moulds as it is very easy to remove the papier mâché from them once it has dried. As long as you follow the guidelines for use given overleaf, your original mould should remain in perfect condition.

Papier mâché objects need not have the same use as the moulds from which they are made; for example, a bowl or basin is a good basis for a hat. You can change a shape drastically by adding handles, rims, necks, spouts or a lid. Add surface texture by making blips or nodules from pulp and sticking them on when the shape has been released from the mould and is dry. Make other surface decorations from dried pasta shapes (shells, bows and the like) or from string.

Right: An exuberant collection of trays and bowls made from pulped paper, using existing moulds with rims, edges and handles built up over pieces of cardboard attached separately. The primitive patterns in bright coloured paints go well with the eccentric shapes. (Madeleine Child)

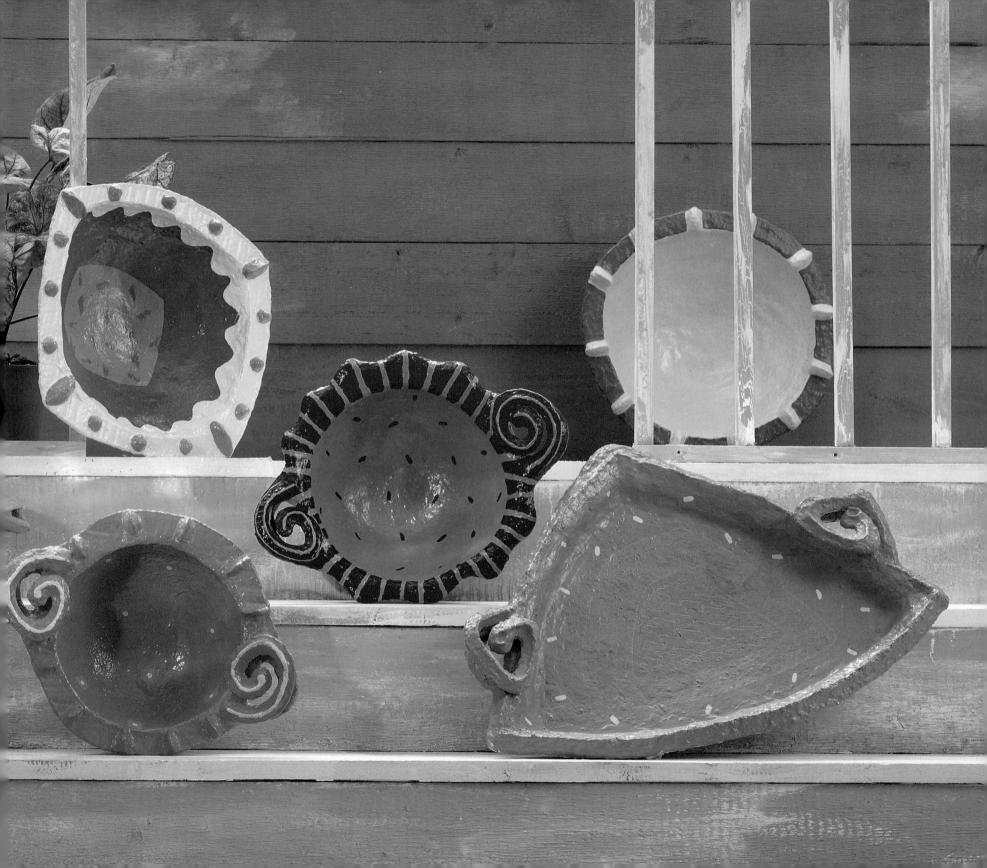

When you are learning to work with pulp, it is best to use wide, shallow moulds such as trays, woks or wide-mouthed bowls, to which the pulp will adhere readily, without slipping off. Pulp shrinks as it dries, so to prevent cracking, place the pulp on the inside of the mould rather than the outside. Keep the layer of pulp thin or it may not dry evenly and may then crack; a thickness of ½in/13mm is recommended. Such a thickness of pulp will be surprisingly strong.

Before adding major embellishments such as handles or necks, draw the shape of your papier mâché object on a sheet of paper a few times, and then draw in the additions you have in mind.

If you have to cut open the papier mâché to release your mould it can be repaired or put together again easily, without any sign of a joint. Just stick the object together with a layer of glue-impregnated paper, then add more pulp as necessary; let it dry and

How to use pulp with a mould

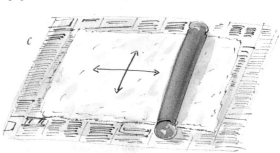

Equipment and materials

Mould — for example, a bowl, tray or wok
Releasing agent, such as petroleum jelly or talcum powder
Newspaper
Plastic bowl
Pulp (see pages 26-7)
Rolling pin

Kitchen paper
Palette knife or spatula
Sandpaper
Cellulose filler/spackle (optional)
Sealer — for example, white glue or gesso (see pages 66-7)
Emulsion paint
Materials for decorating (see pages 54-9)

1 Before you begin, cover your work surface with newspaper. Collect all your tools and materials together. Have a damp cloth nearby to clean your hands as you are working. Fill the plastic bowl with water for the preliminary layer (see step 3).

2 Give the object to be covered a fine coating of the releasing agent — not forgetting edges and rim (a). This will enable you to remove the pulped object easily from the mould once it has dried.

3 To be doubly sure of easy removal from the mould, apply a preliminary coat of paper. Rip some

newspaper into strips and dip in plain water; squeeze out excess water, then overlap the strips on the inside of the greased or powdered mould until it is covered (b). Allow the paper to dry thoroughly.

4a After making the pulp, roll it out with a rolling pin onto a sheet of newspaper (c), then gently lift the pulp and newspaper together. Turn the pulp into the mould; peel away the newspaper.

4b Alternatively, you can apply the pulp in lumps, smoothing it in place with the back of a spoon, your hands or a palette knife (d).

then decorate. This is one of the advantages that papier mâché has over clay.

Before you begin, make sure that you have all your tools and materials around you. Clear a space for working and a space for drying, if possible. If you are working in a cold climate, you will need a direct heat source such as a fan heater or an airing cupboard. In a warm climate, put the object out to dry in the sun — ideally, raised out of harm's way.

Right: Two large varnished bowls and a functional tray, all made from pulped paper on a cardboard base. The bottom bowl has a wavy edge on which blobs of pulp make a relief pattern. The spiral handles are appealing, as is the sgraffito (incised) decoration in bright colours. (Madeleine Child)

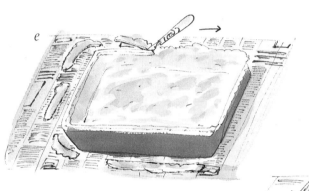

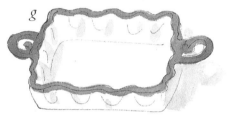

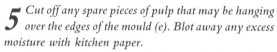

5 *Cut off any spare pieces of pulp that may be hanging over the edges of the mould (e). Blot away any excess moisture with kitchen paper.*

6 *You can make a fancy edge by scoring the pulp with a fork, or pushing with thumb and forefinger in much the same way as decorating pastry (f).*

7 *Leave the object to dry in a warm place, moving it regularly so that it dries evenly. When the object is almost but not completely dry, you can smooth the surface with a palette knife or spatula. Attach handles or other embellishments, using a thin coat of pulp.*

8 *Allow the papier mâché object to dry thoroughly. Remove from the mould. If a smooth finish is desired, sand the object with coarse, then fine sandpaper. Fill any dents or cracks with filler/spackle or apply more pulp. Leave to dry, then sand lightly.*

9 *Seal the object by painting on a thin coat of white glue or a layer of gesso (see pages 66-7).*

10 *When the sealant is dry, apply a background coat of emulsion paint. Allow this to dry.*

11 *Decorate the papier mâché object using one of the methods described on pages 54-9 (g).*

The most widespread method of producing papier mâché objects is layering — that is, building up a gradual accumulation of paper, skin upon skin. This approach offers great versatility of form and decoration, and can be used to create items of delicate beauty, like the bowls and plate shown here.

Layering

PAPER

Layering pieces of paper, or laminating as it is sometimes known, is usually the first craft to which we are introduced as children. This technique allows the creative imagination to take over, resulting in perhaps a utilitarian pot or vase, perhaps a wonderfully expressive puppet or mask. In addition to its ease of use, requiring no specialized technical knowledge or equipment, layering has the added bonus of being ecologically sound, because it encourages the recycling of old newspapers. The layering method is extremely versatile, and can be used to create a vast range of objects, from the functional to the highly ornate.

The importance of drying between each layer of glue and paper should never be underestimated. If the paper is not left to dry between coats, the end-result will be disappointing. The form will probably degenerate, and fungus is likely to occur. It is difficult to give exact drying times, as these are determined by the size of the project, the number of layers of paper, and the weather. Drying may be forced by putting an object in the sun, on a warm radiator, or in the oven on a very low temperature. An object dried in this way will need regular turning to make sure that every surface is dried. If you use an oven, you will need, of course, to watch the piece carefully to make sure that it doesn't burn.

The best method, however, is simply to leave objects to dry with air circulating around them.

Above: In a layered object the layers themselves can play a major part in the decoration. For example, decorative motifs can be allowed to show through tissue paper. Here, patches of newspaper, arranged haphazardly, play an integral part in the design of a striking wall plate. (Carolyn Quartermaine)

Right: These bowls, made from two or three layers of handmade paper built onto moulds, are so delicate that they appear to be constructed from leaves. The top bowl on the right has metallic threads running through it, which help to hold the bowl together but also serve a decorative purpose. The decoration is subtle, using a combination of watercolour and small pieces of silk. The speckles in the paper are created by using various colours of pulp in the vat when actually forming the sheets of paper. (Maureen Hamilton-Hill)

Before starting work, make sure that your paste is in a wide-mouthed container so it is easy to use; this will also help to prevent too much mess.

Most papier mâché artists prefer to use ripped as opposed to cut paper. The best way is to rip along the grain (usually parallel with the longest edge). The strips or squares should be of uniform size, big enough to handle easily. It is best to work with the paper going in one direction on one layer and in the opposite direc-

tion on the next. This not only adds strength but also enables you to see the area you have already covered, ensuring that the surface remains even.

If you wish to use a bowl-shaped mould with a relatively narrow opening, or an otherwise awkward shape, the object will have to be made in two pieces. In this case, follow the steps as for layering a normal mould. When you are finished, use a scalpel to cut the papier mâché object in half for easy removal from the

How to layer on an existing mould

a

b

Equipment and materials

Mould (see pages 48-51)
Releasing agent — for example, petroleum jelly or talcum powder
Newspaper
Damp cloth
Plastic bowl
Thin rubber gloves (optional)
Wallpaper paste

Wide brush
Craft knife
Sealer — for example, white glue or gesso (see page 25)
Emulsion paint
Materials for decorating (see pages 54-9)

1 *Before you begin, cover your work surface with newspaper. Collect all your tools and materials together. Have a damp cloth nearby to clean your hands as you are working and a bowl of water for the first layer.*

2 *Give the object to be covered a fine coating of a releasing agent such as petroleum jelly or talcum powder (a). This will enable you to remove the layered object easily from the mould. Make sure when applying the releasing agent that you coat the edges and the rim.*

3 *To be doubly assured of easy removal from the mould, apply a preliminary coat of unpasted paper. Rip some newspaper into strips and dip them in plain water; squeeze*

out the excess water, then position the strips in overlapping rows on the inside of the greased mould until the entire mould is covered (b). Allow to dry thoroughly.

4 *Repeat step 3, this time dipping the pieces of paper into the paste. Apply the paper in the opposite direction to the first layer. To cover the paper with paste, either dip the pieces into the paste and squeeze off any excess between your fingers, or brush the paste onto the paper with a wide brush. Overlap the pieces as you stick them down, making sure that the first layer of paper is completely covered by the second layer. Allow to dry thoroughly.*

mould. Join the two halves together with papier mâché, allowing each additional layer to dry thoroughly; finish in the normal manner.

You may not wish to remove the mould over which you are layering, but instead keep it as an integral part of the finished project. If so, do not add the releasing agent or the first coat of water-soaked paper. Before you begin, sand the surface on which you are layering; papier mâché adheres best to a rough surface.

These bowls, made from layers of handmade paper built around an existing mould, were created in slightly different ways. For the top two the paper was dyed before construction and the pattern formed by the way in which the paper has been built up. For the bottom bowl, layers of tissue paper were then added to the handmade paper. Other bowls by the same artist are shown on pages 38-9. (Sarah Simpson)

5 Add the next and subsequent layers, making sure that each layer is dry before adding the following layer (c). If your object requires a lid, check that the lid will still fit before adding more layers.

6 When you have as many layers as you require, remove the paper shape from the mould by twisting it (d). If it gets stuck, you may have to cut a little away with a craft knife and repair it with another piece of papier mâché once the object is released.

7 You may wish to add handles, lips or spouts at this stage, making sure they are well secured at the joint (see pages 42-3). Then add a few extra layers of papier

mâché so as to blend in your additions.

8 Seal the object by painting on a thin coat of white glue or a layer of gesso (see pages 66-7). This will give a hard surface to the papier mâché and will prevent any paint from spreading.

9 When the sealant is dry, apply a background coat of emulsion paint. Allow this to dry.

10 Decorate the finished papier mâché object (e).

One of the most versatile moulds you can use is a balloon. Balloons are inexpensive to buy, easy to store, and they come in all sizes so you can choose whether to make a small or large object. If you decide to use the basic round or pear-shaped balloons, you can create vases, bowls, jugs or masks. Long balloons will allow you to make cylindrical vases, or shapes which you can then cut into sections to make bracelets or other items of jewelry.

As with other papier mâché work, the basic requirements are simply glue, newspaper and a work surface, in addition to the balloon. When working with balloons you need not use a releasing agent as the papier mâché comes away from the rubber of the balloon without any difficulties. Allow twelve days to complete a large vase, although this time may vary depending upon the temperature of the area in which the papier mâché is drying. You may wish to start a

How to layer over a balloon

Equipment and materials

Balloon
Sewing thread
Wallpaper (wheat) paste
Newspaper
Scissors
Cardboard
Masking tape, stapler
and staples, or white glue
White emulsion paint
Paintbrushes,
various sizes
Materials for decorating
(see pages 54-9)
Matt polyurethane
varnish

These instructions are for making a papier mâché vase; adapt them to make other objects.

1 *Blow up a balloon and tie a knot in it. Tie a length of sewing thread around the knot (a). Mix the paste with water until it is the consistency of thick cream.*

2 *Rip the newspaper into pieces approximately 4 inches/10cm square. Dip a piece of paper into the paste and stick it onto the balloon, smoothing it into position. Repeat this process with the next piece of paper (b). If you wish, you can overlap the pieces.*

3 *Continue applying newspaper to the balloon, overlapping each piece and keeping the thread free.*

Make sure that you smooth each piece into position as you work. When the balloon is completely covered, hang it from the thread in a doorway or under a table to dry overnight.

4 *The following day, cover the balloon with another layer of paper in the same way; allow this layer to dry thoroughly. Altogether you will need to cover the balloon eight times, allowing each layer to dry thoroughly before applying the next.*

5 *When the eight layers are dry, remove the balloon by untying the knot or popping with a pin. For the top opening of your vase, make a hole in the papier mâché*

production line for your work so that you have some balloons in the early stages of layering and others at the decorating stage. In this way, you can go to a different stage when you tire of the one you are working on. To have a production line going, start a few fresh balloons each day — but make sure you can store them all.

When adding a design, remember that the pot has a back as well as front and sides, which allows plenty of scope for surprises.

These two bowls were made by the technique of layering over balloons. The top bowl is fairly shallow: to make this piece a large proportion of the balloon has been taken away. For the lower bowl, the artist exploited the elasticity of papier mâché by bending the rim inward. The floral decoration is an effective combination of découpage, distressing and paint. (Jane Macartney)

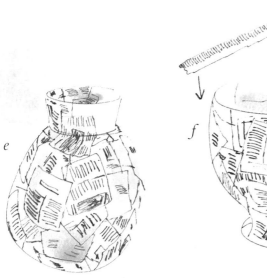

shape either by gently ripping the papier mâché or using scissors to cut an opening. Pull out the balloon (c).

6 You may wish to shape the neck of the vase by adding a lip or funnel. Cut the desired shape from cardboard, then tape, staple or glue the cardboard onto your papier mâché (d).

7 Add at least three layers of papier mâché over the cardboard, both inside and out (e). Allow each layer to dry thoroughly before applying the next.

8 Cut the bottom off the papier mâché vase to make a flat base. Tear strips of newspaper long enough to cover the gap, dip these strips in paste, and smooth across

the opening at the bottom, overlapping each piece (f). Apply at least three layers of papier mâché to the base, allowing each layer to dry thoroughly before applying the next.

9 Paint the inside and the outside of the vase with white emulsion paint before starting to decorate (g). You can decorate the vase in a endless number of ways. Beginners may wish to use acrylic paint or gouache to decorate their early pieces.

10 When the decorated vase is completely dry, apply a coat of matt polyurethane varnish, inside and out.

The whole character and function of an object can be changed by the embellishments added to it. For example, if you have used a bowl as a mould to create the basic papier mâché shape, by adding a rim, handles or a spout you can change the whole concept of the piece.

Handles must usually be sturdy as well as being an attractive addition to a piece. You can use chicken wire for strength, but it is also possible to use flat folded pieces of paper which are glued into place; more layers of paper are then added to make a strong joint where the handle meets the body.

Some artists create embellishments that are distinctively their own — for example, embroidery to neaten the edges of jugs, plates and bowls; indentations along the rim; or decorative nodules (see the bowl on page 67 for an example of this).

If you wish to embellish your own papier mâché vessel, first make a sketch of the object on a piece of paper, then draw a variety of rims, handles or spouts on the vessel in different shapes and sizes to decide on the exact style you'd like to create. When you are happy with the shapes you have drawn, follow

Rims, handles and spouts

Equipment and materials

*Layered or pulped vessel
— a bowl, jug or vase
Pencil and drawing paper
Ruler (for rim)
Pair of compasses
(for rim)
Sturdy cardboard (or
chicken wire) (for handle)
Scissors or craft knife
Masking tape or strong
white glue (for rim)
Pulp (see pages 26-7)*

Rim

1 *Measure the diameter of the vessel to which you are going to add a rim. Using a pair of compasses, draw a circle to this diameter on cardboard. Then, sketch the outline of the rim beyond the drawn circle to the exact size and shape you have chosen. Cut the rim out of cardboard using scissors or a craft knife (a).*

2 *Place the rim over the vessel you are decorating; when you are satisfied with its position, secure the rim to the vessel either by taping or gluing it in place.*

3 *Add pulp to the cardboard rim to secure the joint all around, both inside and out (b). Allow the pulp to dry thoroughly.*

4 *When dry, turn the vessel upside down and add more pulp to the underside of the cardboard, particularly at the join (c). Allow to dry thoroughly.*

5 *Finally, add a thin layer of pulp to the upper side of the rim. Allow to dry thoroughly before decorating.*

the directions below to add a rim or handle. To add a spout, cut a piece of sturdy cardboard into an equilateral triangle shape and fold in half, forming a V; the point of the triangle will be the tip of the spout. Attach the bottom edge of the cardboard triangle to your vessel using masking tape or glue. If the top edge of your vessel rises above the V-shape of the spout, cut away the excess papier mâché using a craft knife. Apply layers of pulp to the join and the cardboard until the spout is entirely covered. Allow to dry thoroughly before decorating.

Unconventional proportions can make the handle an interesting design feature, as shown in these two jugs. Note how the handle colour matches the treatment of the integral spout, and how the two elements are linked by a narrow border along the rim. (Jane Macartney)

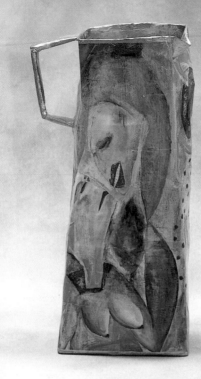

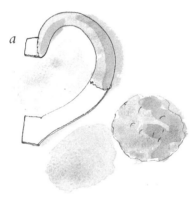

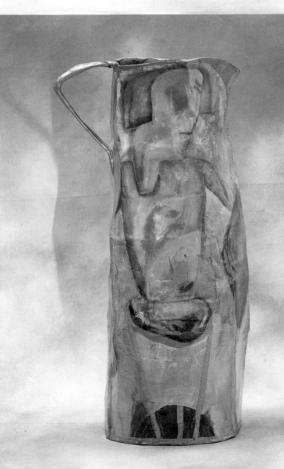

Handle

1 *When you have chosen a handle shape from those you have sketched, make a full-size pattern of it from cardboard, adding two small tabs to the ends of the handle for insertion into the vessel. Alternatively, you can fashion the handle out of chicken wire.*

2 *Apply a thin layer of pulp to the handle shape on both sides, leaving the two tabs that will be inserted into the vessel unpulped as shown (a). Allow the pulp to dry thoroughly.*

3 *Using a craft knife, cut two slots in the vessel in the exact positions where the handle will be inserted.*

4 *Insert the unpulped tabs of the handle into the slots; cover the join smoothly with pulp (b). Allow the pulp to dry thoroughly before decorating.*

Armatures enable you to create a shape rather than have a shape dictated to you by an existing form. An armature is to papier mâché what a skeleton is to the flesh on a human body—its main support. A papier mâché object made with an armature can be any size or take any form, from a large piece of sculpture to a puppet head or piece of delicate jewelry. If you are using pulp, rather than layering, apply a layer of newspaper first, as this will help support the pulp.

An armature should be fairly stable so that it doesn't collapse under the weight of the papier mâché. The simplest armatures can be made by folding and taping newspaper together, and then filling in with yet more paper. Other simple armatures are made by cutting cardboard and stapling or sticking the pieces together with staples or tape. More complex armatures can be constructed from a variety of materials including chicken wire, wood or wire coat hangers.

How to use a wire armature

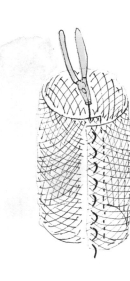

a

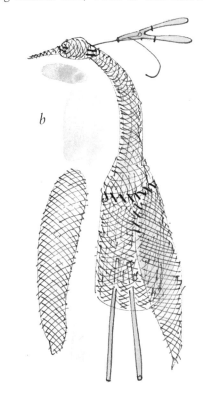

b

Equipment and materials

Visual reference material – for example, drawings or photographs; see step 1
Small-gauge chicken wire
Tin snips/wire cutters
Pliers (optional)
Fine wire
Broomsticks or dowelling for legs (optional)
Cement
Inexpensive plastic flower pot
Mallet
Glue
Newspaper and plain white paper
Wallpaper (wheat) paste
Materials for decorating — for example, paint, dye or antiquing polish (see pages 54-9)
Clear matt polyurethane varnish
Paintbrushes, various sizes

The instructions that follow refer to the construction of the bird pictured here; adapt the step-by-step instructions for making other sculptural forms.

1 *Once you have decided what you wish to make, prepare some visual reference material that you can use while constructing the armature. You can refer to photographs or drawings of the form as you go along, or make a maquette of the finished sculpture.*

2 *Using tin snips/wire cutters, cut a piece of chicken wire to the approximate length you need. If making a body, bend the wire around to make a cylindrical shape, then join the edges together by twisting the wires using a pair of pliers (a).*

3 *The weakest points on a wire armature are the joints; try to keep these to a minimum. Where a joint occurs, either strengthen the joint by overlapping the two pieces of chicken wire or interweave the joint with other pieces of fine wire.*

4 *Cut other pieces of wire for the head and neck. Insert into the body and twist the ends together, again securing the joint firmly (b, top). Add wings and/or arms*

Because no one is going to see the inside of your work, it doesn't matter if the armature is made up of a number of different materials. To join the pieces of an armature together, use staples, tape, wire, nails or screws. A pair of flat-nosed pliers can sometimes help when twisting wire ends together. To balance any top-heavy sculpture, you can make the legs or frame from dowelling or broom handles, then sink the ends into quick-setting cement in a plastic flower pot.

*This **Snakeneck Bird** (height 40 inches/102cm) is made from layers of paper and glue built around an armature. The beak was made from wire, and the legs are billiard/pool cues. The last layers of paper and glue were added in a rough fashion to suggest the features, then the markings of the feathers were added in paint. Matt varnish seals the sculpture. (Priya Commander)*

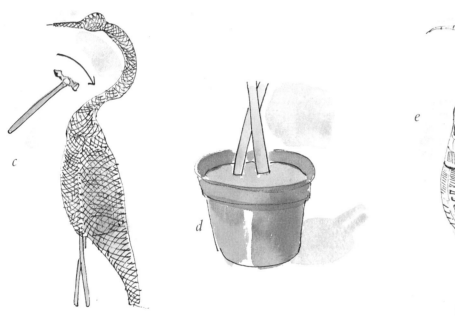

and broomstick or dowelling legs (b, middle, left). Join these onto the body using wire as a reinforcement (b, middle, right).

5 *Refine the skeleton by hammering it into shape, frequently looking at your visual reference (c).*

6 *If necessary, weight the bottom of your armature by securing the broomstick or dowelling legs in cement set in a plastic flowerpot (d).*

7 *When satisfied with the armature, begin applying layers of paper following the directions for layered papier mâché (see pages 36-7), overlapping each piece slightly. Continue until the armature is covered with the* first layer of paper. Allow to dry thoroughly.

8 *Apply a second layer of paper, placing the paper in the opposite direction to the first layer (e). This makes it easier to see where you have worked, and it will also add strength to the form.*

9 *Use white paper for the last papier mâché layer and for the feathers. Partially stick down feather-like strips in the direction that feathers grow.*

10 *When the final layer of paper is thoroughly dry, decorate by painting, dyeing or antiquing (see pages 54-9). Coat the entire sculpture with a clear matt polyurethane varnish to seal.*

The square piece here (shown from both sides) is a colour study for the finished work illustrated opposite, called the **Ranthambhore Tiger.** *This is one of a whole series of tigers, carried out by Katherine Virgils over a long period, that draw upon the significance of the animal in Tibetan culture as a mystical aid to contemplation. As well as referring to the tiger's skin, the stripes evoke fire. The piece (approximately 4ft/ 120cm high) reflects various other preoccupations too — for example, the flattening of a three-dimensional form, and the metamorphosis of nature into a strong architectural outline. One of its companion pieces in the tiger series has been donated to the World Wide Fund for Nature. (Katherine Virgils)*

The methods described over the preceding pages should be taken as starting points only. Artists invent their own methods as they work, until technique and concept become inseparable, absorbed into an evolving style which may become totally instinctive, as natural as breathing.

The pieces shown here are by Katherine Virgils, who has exhibited to great acclaim in Britain, France, Germany, Switzerland, Italy, the USA and the Far East. They are in a highly original idiom that makes use of layered strips of paper, each decorated

Usually, Katherine Virgils begins a piece by pulling out particular papers from her collection. These pieces are torn into strips and decorated before assembly using acrylic and bronze pigments mixed with PVA. Plaster or gesso might also be incorporated, and grains of sand or grit are often added for additional textural interest. Sometimes silver or gold leaf is applied, and sometimes bookbinder's gold. The example here (right) shows the richness achieved by such methods. After decoration the paper is treated with shellac, which protects and varnishes.

individually to create a rich interplay of colour and texture. The pieces reflect a personal response to Indian and Tibetan cultures. Each may incorporate forty or fifty different types of paper, found or bought, ranging from tissue to stiff cardboard — some idea of this variety may be obtained from the central picture here, which shows the underside of one of the pieces. Such a multiplicity of textures contributes to the richness of the work, as each type of surface absorbs paint or dye differently.

A drawing of the design, actual size, is used as a template for cutting out the individual pieces of paper. After decoration the pieces are pinned to a board and adjusted until the overall effect is satisfactory. Finally, the pins are removed and the pieces glued together.

Of course, what an account such as this necessarily fails to convey is the unquantifiable side of the creative process — the artist's passionate, instinctive sense of the rightness of the work as it evolves.

Making your own moulds and templates opens up wide horizons. Original ideas can take shape again and again — with any decorative variations you choose. From small pieces of jewelry to large vessels, the range is endless.

Moulds
AND
TEMPLATES

To create a series of identical objects to your own original design, it will be necessary to make a mould from plaster of Paris. Usually, the interest is on the *inside* of the mould: the concave surface of the inside becomes the convex face of the cast object. Accordingly, the outside of the mould can remain unfinished.

To make your own mould, you need something to cast from. You can form the original shape or model using modelling clay, which is easy to use, doesn't dry up and quite often can be used again. Once you have created this model, make the mould using plaster of Paris. This is bought as a fine white powder; when mixed with water and allowed to stand, it turns into a hard, smooth, white mass.

A template is a re-usable pattern which is used as a guide for cutting out the pieces of a project. Like a mould, it allows you to repeat the same shape over and over again. Templates are most often used in the production of papier mâché jewelry.

Make your master template out of a durable material, such as thick cardboard strengthened with a coat of linseed oil. Once you have made your original template, you can then trace around it to produce as many identical shapes as you need for making layered or pulped papier mâché objects.

You may decide to use papier mâché with other objects such as jewels, sequins, foil and so on. This is where a template can be very useful, providing a backing on which to stick the ornamentation.

Right: A mould, specially made for a project, can take many forms: it can be a re-usable plaster cast, or simply a cardboard cutout made from a template and incorporated in the finished work. These unusual hand mirrors are made from oddments of mirror which have been stuck onto cardboard. The pulped papier mâché was then added to the edge of the mirror, slightly over-lapping to make the frame and the handle. The scalloped shapes were made by pinching the pulp while it was still damp. When dry, the frames were painted with gloss paint. (Madeleine Child)

There are many kinds of plaster of Paris, the best being pottery plaster. Plaster goes bad quickly once the packet is opened, so it is best bought in small quantities.

When mixing plaster, the proportions are 2¾lb of plaster to 1 quart of water (1.25kg to 1 litre). However, you do not need to weigh or measure if you proceed as follows: pour some water into a plastic container. Sprinkle plaster of Paris into the water slowly until a small mound shows just above the surface of the water. Allow the plaster to soak up water for two minutes. Stir with a large wooden spoon until the mixture begins to thicken. Use an even, measured movement; do not whip or you will create air bubbles. The plaster of Paris is then ready to use. Never pour plaster down a sink or it will block the drains: allow it to dry in the plastic bowl, then squeeze the bowl and the plaster will fall off in chunks.

How to make a plaster mould

a

b

c

Equipment and materials

Modelling clay
Craft knife
Plaster of Paris
Water
Mixing bowl
Releasing agent
— petroleum jelly,
talcum powder
Materials for papier
mâché (see pages 24-5)
Materials for sealing,
decorating and finishing
(see pages 24-5 and 54-9)

1 *Fashion the basic shape in modelling clay. Use tools, such as a craft knife, or model freehand (a).*

2 *If you wish the papier mâché object to be a one-sided relief or plaque, or if the object will be the same on both sides, go on to step 3. If the shape is three-dimensional, cut the shape in half lengthwise with a sharp knife, to make a front mould and a back mould. Make sure that the pieces still fit together.*

3 *Thoroughly coat the clay shape with a releasing agent such as petroleum jelly; wipe away any excess with kitchen paper.*

4 *Place the shape on a wooden board or other flat work surface. Make a retaining wall of clay all around and higher than the shape. Make sure that the wall is pressed firmly onto the board (b).*

5 *Mix the plaster. As the mixture starts to thicken, pour a small quantity smoothly over the shape without splashing. Blow the plaster gently onto the shape so that every portion is covered. Continue pouring until the mould is covered. Bang the edge of the work surface to force any air bubbles out.*

6 *Allow to set. First, the plaster will loose its shine, then it will start to harden and become warm. The plaster will then start to cool again. You will know it is set when it is quite cold.* **Note:** *Never force-dry a mould with direct heat, or the plaster will crumble.*

7 *When the plaster is set, remove the retaining wall. Turn the mould over and remove the clay shape (c). Although the mould may appear to be quite hard, allow it to dry out for at least a day.*

This striking plaque was made from layered papier mâché. The original shapes were formed from plasticine/modelling clay which was then covered in a releasing agent. A mould of plaster of Paris was made from each of these shapes. Each mould was then covered in a releasing agent and papier mâché was added by the layering method. The resulting figures were placed in the box to form the composition. The edges of the box were layered in papier mâché and then covered in gold leaf. The rest of the plaque was painted with designer's gouache. (Deborah Schneebeli-Morrell)

d

8 *If you wish to re-use the mould, it would be worth your while to give it a coat of protective varnish (d). Allow plenty of time for the varnish to dry before using the mould. Even if you have applied a coat of varnish, you will still need to apply a releasing agent (see page 28) before using the mould for papier mâché.*

9 *When the mould is ready to use, apply a releasing agent such as petroleum jelly, being careful to cover the edges and to penetrate any little crevices, because otherwise this is where the papier mâché will stick.*

10 *Apply to the mould the pulped (see pages 32-3) or layered (see pages 36-7) papier mâché.*

Colour, pattern and texture are the main elements of decoration. All these can be either integral to the construction (perhaps as the final layer), or applied afterwards. It is fun to mix media — for example, adding beads to vary the texture.

Decorating

Left: These large papier mâché pots (built around chicken wire bases using layers of newspaper and glue) are decorated with precise shapes and bold colours. The design is very strong, a fine example of this artist's style, which he carries over to other media — rugs, stained glass, furniture, paintings. The tallest pot stands four feet (120cm) high. (Malcolm Temple)

There are many more ways to decorate papier mâché than there are methods of making it. Each and every decorative technique that you can dream up is viable, as you will see from the examples of work featured in this book. Although various materials and their basic properties are described over the following pages, the way in which the materials are used is entirely up to the individual craftsman or craftswoman.

For design inspiration go to museums of decorative arts. Textiles in the form of rugs, wall hangings, quilts, embroidery, costumes and accessories are all rich sources of pattern. Ceramics, metalwork and sculpture departments will generate ideas about form. Ethnographic museums will have many examples of pots and masks from various cultures, many of which may translate well into papier mâché. Study the paintings and frames in art galleries; look at the furniture and household artefacts in historic houses and museums. If your interest is wildlife, go to zoos, wildlife parks and natural history museums; draw the shapes of the animals and the markings of their skins, the colours of feathers and scales — even the way the feathers grow. Flowers in vases, gardens or greenhouses, and dried flowers with their subtle faded hues, are all good sources of colour and surface design. Start collecting wrapping paper, greeting cards, candy wrappers, seed packets — anything that you find visually pleasing to use either as the basis for a design or as part of the final decoration.

Keep a notebook of all your ideas and the results so that you can refer to the book for inspiration. If you feel unsure of your artistic skills when it comes to decorating a surface, try the first technique that comes to mind; if you make a mistake, all is not lost. You can simply paint over your mistake with another colour and start again; alternatively, you can add another layer of paper and then redecorate.

Left: This highly decorated bowl is a good example of how papier mâché can be embellished with a combination of materials and techniques, all on the same object. The colours were painted in layers which were then rubbed away to reveal the colours beneath. The red lines were painted boldly in thick acrylic paint. The black patches are pieces of paper stuck in place. The stylized lotuses were inspired by Asian art, in which the lotus is symbolic of a state of enlightenment. To protect a decorated piece such as this, apply two or three coats of clear varnish. (Yanina Temple)

The descriptions on the following pages only touch upon the number of different ways that you can decorate papier mâché. Experiment to find the technique that appeals most to you or to create finishes that aren't even listed here.

Paper finishes

You can finish papier mâché projects with a final coat of ready-printed paper. This can be your own design or commercially printed. You can also use tissue paper as a final layer: you will achieve great depth of colour and contrast in tones where the edges of tissue paper overlap. For a geometric finish, use graph paper for the final layer; one artist has even used crossword puzzles, to bold ends.

You may wish to construct the actual object from special paper, such as handmade paper or fine tissue paper. This type of paper is best used to make simple objects such as bowls, where the beauty lies more in the materials than in the finished form. If you are using tissue or hand-made papers, you will need a very strong glue, such as undiluted white glue (see page 24), to give the necessary strength to the object.

Tracing paper

If you feel that your drawing skills are lacking, you can trace motifs from any surface such as wall tiles, fabric, books or even pieces of china. Place the tracing paper over the image, being careful to cover the image fully. Trace onto the paper using a medium pencil; anything softer may smudge. Repeat your tracing as many times as required. Colour in the design using pencils or felt tip pens, then use the paper as the final layer of your papier mâché.

Photocopies

Photocopying machines can be used to produce repeats of designs. If you do not have access to a colour photocopier, make a line drawing, photocopy it and then colour the motifs by hand. Use this coloured paper for the final layer of papier mâché.

Printing

Using paint or ink, you can print directly onto the surface of a papier mâché object using ready-made, purchased printing blocks or blocks made from carved lino (see pages 62-3), vegetables, cork or pencil erasers. The other way to use a print on papier mâché is to make a block by one of these methods, print sheets of paper with it, then use the printed sheets of paper as your final papier mâché layer.

Découpage

Découpage is the art of decorating a surface with illustrations cut from newspaper, wrapping paper, magazines, postcards and the like. The shapes are cut out and sometimes coloured, then arranged and glued onto a prepared surface. The surface may be plain or painted with a pattern. The découpage is then given about 20 coats of varnish. Often the end-result looks as though it has been either painted or inlaid.

Embossing and relief

You can use a variety of artefacts on papier mâché to produce a raised surface. This can be done as the final finish, or underneath the last coat of paper to give a raised form. String, seeds, beans, bits of cut cardboard and tissue paper, can all be used in papier mâché to add interest to the surface. Plastic animals, small toys, seashells, beads, lace, cloth, metal, leather and embroidery can also be used to decorate papier mâché. Pieces of coloured glass and broken china or mirror, grouted onto the top of a finished object, will make an interesting surface. Use vegetable glue for attaching fabric trims; white glue is best for heavier objects.

Painting

The entire range of paints and pigments — from water colours, gouache paints, oil paints, enamels and acrylics to felt tip pens, pencils and dyes — may be used on papier mâché. For an opaque finish, use gouache. If you require a gradation of shade and tone, transparent watercolours or powdered dyes are excellent. For a glossy finish use either a gloss paint or quick-drying enamels.

You may wish to produce a patterned surface. You can paint simple wavy lines or zigzag patterns; circles, ellipses, dots, triangles and diamonds are all easy to paint and make pleasing patterns. Great variety can be achieved depending on where and how you apply the motifs.

Far left, top: Calligraphy, gold paint and collage techniques (using silk and tissue paper) are incorporated in the plate shown in detail here. The layering allows different levels of decoration to interact, forming a complex pattern. (Carolyn Quartermaine)

Far left, middle: This bowl was made from handmade paper and small strips of silk layered to form a collage. It is in the varying thicknesses and textures, together with the randomness of the arrangement, that the beauty of this design lies. (Maureen Hamilton-Hill)

Far left, bottom: Another detail of a bowl, this time made with thicker, heavier handmade paper, again combined with silk. Holes torn into the structure are a key part of the design. (Maureen Hamilton-Hill)

Pages 56-7: These bowls were water-gilded and then burnished, distressed or oxidized. (Caroline Gibbs)

Many of the home decorating techniques that have had a revival in recent years can also be used to decorate papier mâché, such as dragging, bagging, ragging, spattering, stencilling and marbling, as described below. For more information on these techniques, consult one of the many specialist books in this field — and then experiment.

Wax

This is a very simple "resist" method of decorating. Create a pattern by drawing on the surface of the papier mâché with a wax crayon or candle. Paint the surface with ink or a watercolour wash. The ink or wash will not penetrate the wax, so some areas will be the colour of the wax, and others will be the colour of the ink or wash.

Masking fluid

This is a resist method of decorating which looks a little like batik in its results. Paint parts of the object with masking fluid, then paint the entire object with colour when the masking fluid is dry. When the paint is dry, remove the masking fluid and the masked area will be the background colour. Drop, flick or trail the masking fluid onto the papier mâché, or draw it on in a pattern, for an unusual effect.

Dyes

Powdered dyes may be mixed with pulp to produce unusual hues; keep in mind that the dye will appear lighter when the pulp dries out. For a mottled effect use batches of dyed pulp with undyed pulp or a combination of the two. You can paint dyes onto gesso to produce interesting effects. Because dyes tend to seep into paper and bleed, they can be used to good effect if a free style of decoration is required. Always wear rubber gloves when working with dyes.

Glazing

Glazes can be used for painting, ragging, bagging and sponging. A glaze is a transparent layer of colour (pure pigment suspended in a clear medium), laid thinly over an opaque surface. Oil glazes, known as scumble glazes, are available from good decorating and hardware stores. They dry to a sleek, transparent finish. You can also buy emulsion glazes which are

Right, top: The vibrant colours of this piece reflect the artist's delight in her encounter with India. The paper has been painted with pigments modified by the addition of gesso, as well as by subtle touches of crayons, oils, pastels and pencils, followed by more layers of paint. The grittiness comes from sand applied with the paints. Additional textural interest has been provided by incising through the paint. (Katherine Virgils)

Right, middle: A detail from a scrolled wall-piece, with inset mirror. The pattern has been drawn onto paper, photocopied and then hand-coloured. A wash has been applied over the top, and the colours allowed to run into one another. (Jennie Neame)

Right, bottom: The decoration on this bowl is a combination of paint, collage and pattern scratching. The juxtaposition of bold blocks of paint with speckled and dotted effects is particularly successful. (Yanina Temple)

water-based and dry more quickly than oil-based glazes, and have a fresh, irregular quality.

Mix your glaze with artist's oils the day before you need to use it, as this allows the glaze to become amalgamated and clarified. Work in a well-ventilated, dust-free environment as the glaze will give off fumes and pick up any dust particles in the air. Paint the glaze onto your papier mâché, and allow it to dry for 12-24 hours. Resist premature handling to avoid fingerprints.

Bagging

This technique uses different kinds of bags — both brown paper and plastic — to provide your papier mâché object with great surface depth created by a mottled effect. Paint a glaze all over the object, then dip a bag into turpentine; dab the bag onto the glaze. Change bags as your working bag becomes clogged with paint so that you do not put paint back onto your papier mâché.

Sponging

You can create subtle or highly contrasting effects with sponging, depending on the colours you use and the method of application. Although natural sponges are best, they are quite expensive; you might prefer to use a synthetic sponge cut into pieces, a loosely woven cloth or kitchen paper. Dip your sponging medium into the palest paint colour first, wipe off excess paint with a piece of newspaper, then use a light dabbing motion to transfer the paint to your papier mâché object. Try not to smudge the paint. If you are going to use more than one hue, leave plenty of space for subsequent hues; always use a clean sponge for each separate application. Apply your paints from lightest to darkest, filling in any gaps that are left with the final colour. If you feel that the piece is too dark when you have finished, allow the paint to dry, then apply another coat of the light paint.

Ragging

Ragging is a way to create a randomly mottled effect by removing (or, if you prefer, adding) colour. Have plenty of old cloths handy so that you can discard them as they become clogged with paint. Brush a glaze (or paint) onto the surface of your papier mâché object. Dampen your cloth with turpentine, bunch it up and dab it on the glazed surface. Try not to over-work your piece or you will lose the crispness of the marks you have made.

Marbling

Because water and oil do not mix, an oil-based paint poured onto water will float on the surface. If you place a sheet of paper on the paint-covered water, the paper will acquire a beautiful marbled effect; this paper can then be used as the final layer of your papier mâché. Wear rubber gloves while you work, cover your work area, and have plenty of turpentine and detergent on hand for cleaning up after you're finished.

To make marbled paper, pour about 4 inches/ 10cm of water into a container that is slightly larger all around than your paper. Then mix each paint colour with some turpentine to help the colour spread on the water. Pour one or more paint colours into the water and allow all the paint droplets to come to the surface. Swirl the paint with a stick, a comb, or the end of a paintbrush to create an attractive pattern. Place a sheet of paper gently on the surface of the water, then lift it up carefully to see your marbled design. Allow the paper to dry thoroughly before using it.

Spattering

For an effect similar to that of an "action" painting, try spattering. First, cover all surrounding surfaces including walls, carpets and furniture, because the paint is apt to fly everywhere. A large cardboard box used as a shield will help to contain the volleys of paint. Place the papier mâché object in the middle of the protected area, dip the end of a brush or stick into paint, and sharply flick the paint onto your object. Alternatively, stroke the bristles with a piece of cardboard pulled toward you. Flick from all angles. If the blobs of paint become too thick, blot them carefully using kitchen paper. You can spatter using a succession of different colours to build up a busy pattern.

Spraying

This technique is used to achieve a fine, dotty, slightly misty surface. You can use an airbrush if you have one, or an inexpensive diffuser.

Far left, top: In this detail of a papier mâché monster, the latticework has been cut with a scalpel into a piece of flat cardboard, attached to the papier mâché and coloured with yellow gouache and red felt tip pen. Below this network the surface is textured with green leather and stuck-on mustard seeds. A painted length of plastic-coated wire separates the contrasting areas. (Billy Nicholas)

Far left, middle: Papier mâché can be twisted and turned to make an elaborate relief, as in this section of a mirror frame. The decoration combines paintwork and, to make the crisscross pattern, pyrography (controlled burning). (Kate Sheppard)

Far left, bottom: A detail from the lifelike tail of a fish sculpture. The tail was scored down its length and painted with two coats of different colours. Then the surface was rubbed with fine sandpaper, and specks of gold paint added, to catch the light. (Louise Vergette)

Metallic finishes

For a painted metallic finish, use gold, silver, bronze or copper paints which can be bought in a liquid form and painted onto papier mâché. For a slightly different effect, gold and silver leaf can be applied over a coat of varnish when it is at the stage of being almost, but not quite, dry. Gold and silver leaf are bought in sheets of pure metal or in a synthetic form.

Antiquing

You can make a surface look old by putting on a dark pigment and then wiping most of it off. The dark pigment stays in the cracks and crevices of the surface and accentuates the texture. Add a second or even a third colour so that a rich pattern emerges. You can also use a commercial antiquing polish.

Crackling

An object can be made to look old by introducing fine lines or cracks on top of the finished decorated surface. Crackling is achieved by painting two different media, each with a different drying time, onto an object; one medium is water-based, while the other is oil-based. The different drying times will cause the painted surface to crackle.

You can also use a ready-made crackle varnish. First paint a design using acrylic paints; make sure that the motif you have chosen is suitable for an aged finish. Allow the painted design to dry thoroughly. Then, following the manufacturer's instructions, paint on the crackle varnish.

An airbrush gives more control, but requires experience before you can control it successfully. Altering the distance you hold it from the paper will vary the effect produced. You can also adjust the rate of flow by altering the pressure on the control button. After using an airbrush it is vital to clean it correctly by emptying, refilling with water, squirting water through the nozzle and dismantling again. All traces of colour must be removed carefully.

Stencils

With spraying or spattering, you can mask off an area of the paper with stencils. This allows you to make overlapping patterns in a number of colours.

Right, top: A detail of a peaked hat, with an unusual design of cut-out holes and primitive images formed by pyrography (treatment with a woodburning tool). The cat is jumping to catch the moon. Many coats of varnish make this more helmet than hat. (Kate Sheppard)

Right, middle: Metallic finishes can be used to give substance to papier mâché artefacts. The first step is to coat the papier mâché with several layers of gesso, which is sanded to a smooth finish. Then a layer of colour is added, and on top of that a layer of metal foil. Distressing the resultant surface with wire wool allows the colour to partially show through, contrasting with the gold or silver. (Caroline Gibbs).

Right, bottom: This papier mâché bowl was covered in a layer of gesso, which was sanded and then painted with bole — a coloured clay. Each layer was sanded before the application of further layers. (Carey Mortimer)

Lino CUTS

Lino cut printing is one of the most popular block printing methods. Essentially, it is a 20th-century development of the woodcut, substituting linoleum for wood. The tools you need are widely available, and can be used to make inventive designs to decorate papier mâché.

The lino cut technique is an ideal way to create bold, graphic patterns. These papier mâché plates and bowls illustrate the kind of effect you can achieve. They have all been made by layering white paper and glue onto bowls and plates covered in clear plastic wrap/saran wrap. When dry the wrap was removed. To decorate the pieces, a fish design was cut out of lino and printed as a series of images onto white paper. The fish images were then cut out and stuck onto the bowls and plates. Modifying the effect with additional decorative devices — in this case spirals, dots and dashes, applied by brush — provides variety within the same basic pattern and palette. (Melinda While)

Block printing is an effective way to cover a papier mâché object with pattern. It is yet another craft that you can do at home without recourse to expensive equipment. Both large- and small-scale work can be decorated in this manner. One simple method of block printing involves the use of an ordinary rubber stamp and ink pad. For more personal designs, you can carve patterns into lino, rubber, cork, vegetables or wood, or incise a design onto metal.

If you are planning to print on a curved object, keep the motif small or use a rubber stamp which can curve around the surface. Another effective and versatile method of decorating curved surfaces is to print onto a piece of paper, then tear or cut the paper and use it to construct the final layer of your papier mâché project.

Lino printing lends itself to simple, bold motifs. The image is cut into the lino using special tools — lino cutters — designed for that purpose. If you use lino-printed paper on a papier mâché object, as opposed to printing directly onto the piece, you can arrange the images as you wish — close together, spaced out in sequences, or perhaps as a bold frieze encircling a pot or vase.

Lino cutting and printing are easy, particularly if you are printing in only one colour. The design is transferred from tracing paper onto the lino, and the image is then carved out using special tools (see next page). Then, ink is applied to the raised surfaces left by the cutting, and the image is transferred to the paper. The print will be a mirror image of your lino block; keep this in mind when printing numbers or letters.

If you wish to print a whole sheet of paper with a repeat design, first divide the paper into rectangles of the same size as your lino block. Print onto every other rectangle so that you have plenty of room to work without smudging the next repeat. When you have completed the first half of the design go back and fill in the rest in the same way.

To print in two colours, first draw the full colour design on paper. Then, trace each separate coloured section on separate pieces of tracing paper. Cut two pieces of lino the same size. Transfer the lines of the first colour onto one piece of the lino and the second colour onto the other piece. Then, carefully carve the lines of each design into the lino. Mark the back of each block with either a number or the name of the colour to be printed so that you do not pick up the wrong block by mistake. Print your first colour, making registration marks by drawing the perimeter of the block on the paper with a pencil. When the first colour is dry, print the second colour by matching up the perimeter of the block to the marks left by the first block. Print light hues first, then dark ones. You can create a three-colour print by overlapping areas on both blocks. If you print blue over yellow, you will obtain green; blue over red will make purple; red over yellow will make orange.

You can make a lino block, and thus a print, using just one type of cutter; however, this will probably result in a monotonous image. Ideally you should purchase one handle and a variety of cutters to fit into the handle. Use your tools with care and always follow the instructions given below.

It is vitally important that your cutters are sharp and therefore easy to use. Always cut away from your body, not towards it. The V-shaped cutting tool,

called a divider, leaves a V-shaped groove which prints as a line. To use this tool, hold the ball of the handle in the palm of your hand; using your thumb as a guide, push the cutter into the lino, smoothly following the lines of your design and removing a shred of lino to leave a neat groove. Gouges, or U-shaped tools, will make a wide line. Very thick gouges are used for removing large areas of lino.

The lino should be thick. If you are going to

How to make a lino print

Equipment and materials	Plywood or soft wood;
	wood glue (optional)
Newspaper for covering	Rubber roller (or wooden
work surface	mallet if using wood and
Tracing paper	wood glue)
Pencil for drawing	Piece of thick glass
Soft lead pencil	or formica/plastic
White poster paint	laminate
Paint brush	Lino ink
Lino	Paper on which to print
Lino cutters	Adhesive tape

1 Cover your work surface with newspaper. Draw your design on paper.

2 Trace the design with a pencil, then turn the tracing paper over. Go over the design visible through the back of the tracing paper, with a soft lead pencil.

3 Because lino is dark, it is difficult to see pencil lines marked on its surface, so first paint the lino with a thin coat of white poster paint. When the poster paint is dry, tape your design, soft-pencil-side down, onto the white side of the lino. Go over your design with a pencil, transferring the design to the lino (a). Remove the tracing paper, taking

care not to smudge the image.

4 Use lino cutters to cut out the lines of the design (b). To cut curves, turn the block, keeping the tool firmly in your hand. When the block is cut, wash off the remaining poster paint with a damp cloth. Allow the lino to dry.

5 If you are making a block to keep or use repeatedly, stick on a piece of plywood or soft wood, using wood glue. This should be about ½in/1cm thick.

6 Squeeze lino ink onto a piece of glass or formica/plastic laminate. Then roll the rubber roller over the ink until it is thinly and evenly spread (c).

use the same block many times, it is worth mounting it on a wooden block approximately ½in/1cm thick; this will make it easier to handle. Although a printing press is the best way to transfer the image from the block to the paper, a wooden mallet banged on the back of the block will suffice. If your lino isn't mounted on wood, run a roller over the back of the lino a few times to transfer the design. Patchiness is a quality of lino prints: do not strive for perfect neatness.

This "service" of fish plates has been made in the same ways as the plates on the previous pages, but with the tones reversed. The middle plate has the interesting addition — a pattern made by an Indian woodcut normally used for fabric printing. For a striking decorative effect, sketchy lino prints can be combined with bold hand painting. (Melinda While)

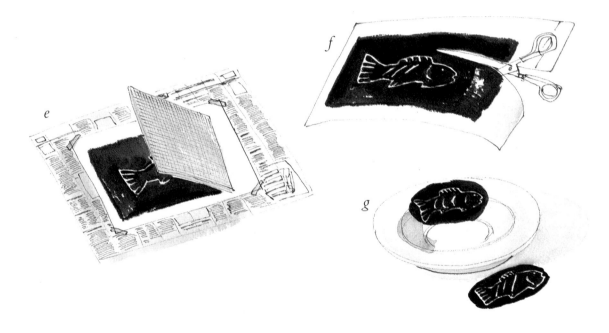

7 *Using the roller, apply the ink to the lino block (d). Do not lift the roller until it has travelled the whole length of the block. If bubbles form, you have probably not smoothed the ink thinly enough on the glass, or the ink may be too thick.*

8 *Carefully rub any ink out of the incised areas of the block with a cloth.*

9 *Place the paper you wish to print face upward on your work surface; tape it at the corners. Place the lino block, inked side down, on the paper. If the lino is not attached to a wood block, run a clean roller firmly over the* back of the lino to transfer the design to the paper. If the lino is secured to a wooden block, hit the back of the block with the wooden mallet. Lift up the lino carefully (e).

10 *Continue until you have as many prints as you need. When you have finished, wash your tools and lino block in warm soapy water.*

11 *After your lino prints are dry, tear or cut them into strips (f).*

12 *Apply the prints to your papier mâché object as the final layer of paper (g).*

How to use gesso as a base

In the late 17th and 18th centuries, gesso was used as moulded decoration on chairs, mirror frames and the legs of pier tables, and was often gilded. For producing the exuberant curlicues popular during the Rococo period, it was found to be easier to model gesso on a wire base than to carve the designs from wood.

You can make your own gesso as described below, or alternatively you can purchase it in a liquid form. After using gesso, soak any brushes in warm water immediately afterwards for ten minutes; then wash the brushes in soapy water and dry thoroughly.

When gesso dries, it becomes as hard as stone and can be sanded smooth to a porcelain-like appearance; that is why it is often used as a coating prior to painting. Gesso not only strengthens papier mâché but dramatically changes its appearance. When you are applying gesso, an uneven or textured papier mâché surface can be an advantage: if the papier mâché is too

Equipment and materials	Wire balloon whisk
	Decorator's brush
Mould	Coarse and fine
Releasing agent — for	sandpaper
example, petroleum jelly	Wooden block
or Talcum powder	Thin metal strips for
Paper	decoration
Wallpaper paste	Powdered tempera paint
Ground chalk (whiting)	or gilding materials
or gypsum (plaster of	Lino cutter for carving
Paris)	Balsa wood for nodules
Rabbit-skin size	Cellulose-based varnish
Double saucepan	Wire wool

1 Grease the inside or outside of the mould, and the rim, with the releasing agent (see page 36, step 2)

2 Tear your paper into strips. Apply a preliminary coat of plain paper for easy removal from the mould (see page 36, step 3); allow to dry thoroughly. Mix the wallpaper paste according to the manufacturer's instructions.

3 For the second layer, dip the strips of paper into the paste. Lay the strips in the opposite direction to the first layer, overlapping and smoothing them in place. Allow to dry thoroughly.

4 Continue adding layers until you have built up 10 to 12 layers, allowing each layer to dry thoroughly before adding the next. When the last layer has dried, remove the piece from the mould by twisting (see page 37, step 6).

5 Mix one part rabbit-skin size (which comes in granule form) to 15 parts water; soak in a bowl overnight.

6 Heat the soaked rabbit-skin size in a double saucepan; do not boil.

7 Add the chalk or gypsum to the mixture and whisk with a wire balloon whisk, until the mixture is the consistency of double/heavy cream (a).

smooth the gesso may crack. If this does happen, simply apply further coats of gesso. Gesso can be coloured by adding (tempera) powder paint to the mixture, or its hardened surface can be painted.

The pots featured here show the use of papier mâché covered with gesso that has been either inlaid with copper or pewter, or gilded and scratched. In the lower example, the surface has been embellished with small horns and nodules, like a Viking helmet.

These two papier mâché bowls both include gesso in their construction. The top one has strips of copper inlaid, and the inside edge patterned in lead pencil. The lower pot has water-gilded horns or spikes around its outside, made from balsa and then covered in gesso after gluing. The pattern on the outside is cut into the gesso and coloured. (Carey Mortimer)

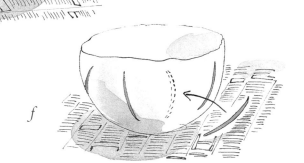

8 *If lumps develop you can sieve the mixture before you apply it. As the mixture cools it becomes thicker and hardens; if it becomes too thick before you finish, gently reheat it.*

9 *Paint the gesso onto the papier mâché, both inside and out (b). Allow to dry thoroughly.*

10 *Sand the gesso, first with coarse sandpaper wrapped around a block, then with fine sandpaper (c).*

11 *To add nodules, carve conical shapes from balsa wood; apply glue to the base of each nodule and stick onto the object (e). When the glue beneath each nodule is dry, paint another coat of gesso onto the whole object to form a continuous surface, then paint or gild.*

12 *Decorate by painting, gilding or carving a design directly into the gesso using lino cutters (d).*

13 *To decorate with copper or pewter, press the thin metal strips onto the final coat of gesso while still wet; rub more gesso over the edges of the metal to secure (f).*

14 *Apply a cellulose-based varnish as a final coat. After it dries, you can make the surface matt by rubbing with wire wool.*

INTERIORS

Bowls and pots in papier mâché, made in approximate imitation of ceramic shapes, provide an unmissable opportunity for flamboyant decoration. The basic construction techniques are very easy.

Colourful

PAPER POTS

Large narrow-necked vases or round-bellied pots present a generous surface area that cries out for bold decorative motifs; whereas on shallow bowls it is often the concave inside surface that offers itself readily for ornamentation. Instead of an all-over pattern you might consider adding one or two isolated images — such as stylized fish. To protect the decoration of your pot, be sure to add two or three coats of varnish.

Possible vase shapes include the sphere, the baluster shape (bulging like an architectural baluster), the Chinese stem cup and the tall "sleeve" vase.

You might decorate in blue and white, using pseudo-Chinese motifs, or copy the polychrome palette used in Renaissance Italy and Spain on tin-glazed earthenware (maiolica). The bold, geometric motifs of Art Deco pottery are another rich source of inspiration, sanctioning the use of a "hot" palette.

Similar decorative approaches can be taken to plates, plaques and other pottery forms.

Left: This miscellany of bowls make bold use of colour and pattern. They are multilayered, their base colours rubbed, scribbled upon or distressed. Notice the use of motifs within motifs. (Yanina Temple)

Pages 68-9: Papier mâché lights, frames and vessels can be used in novel ways to transform an interior. These pieces differ enormously in shape and function, but all reflect the artist's style. (Louise Vergette)

Above: A detail from a large papier mâché pot made by layering over a framework. The pot shows strong use of colour (gouache) and a striking pattern of geometric forms. (Malcolm Temple)

There is a long tradition of treating pottery and porcelain plates and other "flatware" as a base for high-quality decoration — flowers, landscapes, chinoiseries (pseudo-Chinese scenes) and portraiture are just some of the subjects that have proved popular. You can take a similar approach in papier mâché, deriving your designs from ceramic precedents or inventing new ornamentation of your own.

Plates can be made in a shallow mould such as a wok, but the easiest way is to use a ceramic plate, layering on its upper surface. A sheet of plastic wrap/saran wrap makes an excellent releasing agent — all you do is lift the wrap off the ceramic surface and the

layered plate will come away with it. A footring can be added afterwards if you wish.

Another method is to use a template of cardboard. Cut out a circle the size you want the plate to be, then cut V-shaped slits around the circumference. Close the gaps together using masking tape, or a staple gun. Now layer papier mâché on both sides of this construction.

A separate rim can be added after you have formed the main shape. Attach a cut piece of cardboard and layer over the whole plate, body and rim.

To give your papier mâché plates a personal significance, it is worth decorating them as commemorative items — for example, to celebrate a birth or wedding or anniversary. A calligraphic inscription could be added as part of the last layer of paper. It would be easy to add a portrait by photocopying a photograph. However, great care would be needed to prevent this from looking too contrived — a simple silhouette might work better, cut out from paper against a contrasting background. Ephemera of personal significance could also be built into the design — in much the same way as patchwork quilt makers use scraps of fabric that serve to remind them of previous homes and beloved relatives.

The surface design on the papier mâché plates and cone in this photograph are a signature of this artist's work. The pieces are made from layers of newspaper and glue, and the decoration combines paper collage (with tissue paper), silks, gold patterning and calligraphy. The uniform palette, in which the same hues are employed in different proportions (note the minimal red in the right-hand example), gives the plates a matching appearance despite the differences of pattern. (Carolyn Quartermaine)

With papier mâché you can turn throwaway items of packaging into cherishable objects that might look good, for example, on an occasional table or a dressing table. Or, for perhaps greater satisfaction, you can take as your starting point boxes you have made yourself.

Boxes

Boxes are seen as magical objects because they often contain surprises. However, as you can see from the examples featured here, the original purpose may become almost irrelevant: these boxes have become objects to be cherished and desired in their own right. The shape, design and method of decoration are what gives a box its distinctive character.

Some of the earliest products to be made commercially out of papier mâché were boxes. In India, papier mâché boxes were originally produced to package expensive items such as Kashmir shawls and gift packets of tea. Small papier mâché boxes are still being made in Kashmir for holding cigars, stationery, powder, coasters and other items. Commercially made papier mâché boxes take many forms including animals, fish and birds.

One approach is to cover existing cardboard boxes with handmade paper and then make lids to fit them. Note that handmade papers are subtle and delicate, and need to be featured in a simple setting if they are not to lose their intrinsic qualities.

Embossing can be used to give decorative emphasis to the lid: for example, the highly ornamental box here (left) incorporates string to create a raised surface. Padded linings, like miniature pieces of upholstery, add an attractive sense of luxury.

Left: Richly decorated boxes are ideal for jewelry. This one is balsa wood covered in layers of paper and glue. The raised design is of string stuck on the lid; it has been covered with more layers of paper and glue before being decorated. (Jo Dixon)

Above: Old cardboard boxes can be transformed by a papier mâché covering. Here, the final, decorative layer is of handmade papers which have been stuck down, and varnished after the application of a fabric protector. (Maureen Hamilton-Hill)

The original shape of a box need not dictate the final form of your papier mâché object. You can construct an armature around the box to create almost any shape you wish. You can add surface nodules and bumps in the form of lumps of glue-impregnated tissue or kitchen paper. Or you can make a free-standing relief to stand on the lid.

To make your own box, first draw the basic pattern on cardboard; this should include a base and the four adjacent sides. Cut out the shape using scissors or a craft knife. Then, using the craft knife, score the box along the lines where it will be folded; score by running your craft knife along the lines, cutting into, but not all the way through, the cardboard. Fold the sides up and join together carefully using tape. You can now begin to papier mâché the box. Layer a piece of paper onto the base for strength. When the first layer of paper has dried, you

How to make a box with a lid

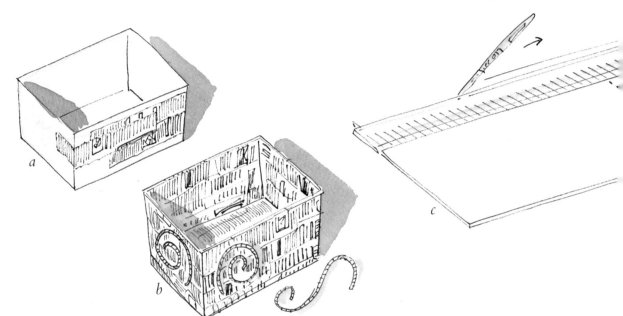

Equipment and materials

White glue
Wide-necked container
for glue
Newspaper
Cardboard box, any size
Emulsion paint
Craft knife
Scissors
Ruler
Pencil

Thin cardboard
Paintbrushes,
various sizes
Materials for decorating
— for example, paint,
string, tissue paper,
handmade paper
Water-repellent spray
(optional)
Matt polyurethane
varnish

The following instructions explain how to treat a ready-made cardboard box with papier mâché and construct your own lid. White glue is recommended: wallpaper paste tends to be wetter and is more likely to distort the cardboard shape underneath.

1 Pour the glue into a wide-necked container. Rip the paper into strips each measuring about 1 x 2 inches/ 2.5 x 5cm.

2 Dip the first paper strip into the glue and run it between your thumb and forefinger to remove excess glue. Wrap the paper around the outside of the box, smoothing it carefully in place (a).

3 Apply the second piece of paper as you did the first, dipping it in glue, removing the excess glue and slightly overlapping the first piece.

4 Continue in this manner until the whole of the box has been covered, both inside and out. Allow to dry thoroughly before applying the next layer; apply at least three layers.

5 If you want to decorate the box with a raised design, dip string into white glue and arrange it in a pattern (b), then apply another layer of paper over the string. When the top layer is completely dry, coat all surfaces of the box with emulsion paint to seal it.

can either pulp or layer papier mâché all over the box.

If your box already has a lid, you must be careful about the number of layers or depth of pulp you apply: otherwise the lid may no longer fit the box when you have finished. As the work progresses, but only when both the base and the lid are dry, try fitting the lid on the box. Before the lid becomes too tight to move easily, make sure that you stop layering or pulping in the area of overlap.

Balsa wood is the basis for all the papier mâché boxes shown here. A relief pattern has been created on the lids by applying string, and then more papier mâché over the top. Acrylic paints, gouache, inks and crayons applied in rich patterns show the influence of the artist's travels in India. The boxes are lined with handpainted silks, the hues harmonizing, inside and out. (Jo Dixon)

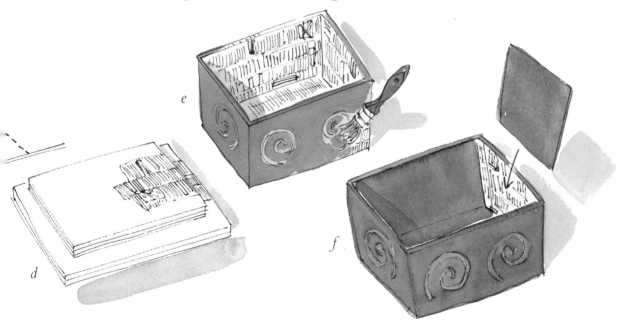

6 *When the paint is dry, you will be able to ascertain the final thickness of the box in order to make the lid. Measure the outer dimensions of the box and draw them on the thin cardboard.*

7 *Using scissors or a craft knife, cut out the cardboard (c) and place it on top of the box. It should fit exactly. Cut another piece of cardboard to the same size and glue to the first piece, matching all edges.*

8 *Measure the internal dimensions of the box and cut another piece of thin cardboard slightly smaller than these measurements. Cut two more pieces of cardboard the same size and glue them on top of one another, so there*

are three layers in all. Centre this small thick piece of cardboard on the double piece you first cut; glue in place. Allow to dry thoroughly, then check the fit.

9 *Layer paper over the lid, mitring the corners to prevent bulky edges (d). Add at least three layers, then apply a coat of emulsion paint to seal it.*

10 *If you are using handmade, tissue or other decorative paper, spray with water repellent after the paper has dried.*

11 *Coat the outside with polyurethane varnish (e). When the varnish is dry, decorate the inside of the box — for example, with fabric (f).*

A frame must be pleasing in its own right, whether it be visually set apart from the picture or mirror, or integral to the whole. Papier mâché is the ideal medium to make sculptural, expressive frames, in styles that would be much more difficult to achieve in wood.

Frames

Left: Gilded swathes of cloth and braid appear draped around a somewhat overwhelmed pot plant! This is in fact a double mirror frame made from layers of paper and glue stuck onto a chicken wire skeleton. The decoration includes duplicated images of a vase of flowers, produced on a photocopier, and carefully embellished with handpainting. (Jennie Neame)

Right: This papier mâché frame seems almost alive with its mass of snake-like forms, undulating in and out of entwined stylized flowers. Despite its intricacy, the frame is strong and works well for the function for which it is intended. (Kate Sheppard)

Frames, as with other forms of applied decoration, reflect the time in which they were made. As papier mâché is a medium that does not dictate its own finished appearance, it may be used to produce frames in any style from any period of history. Frames may be smooth and flat, covered in gesso and gold leaf, or lacquered and painted; or, alternatively, they may be decorated in relief with the forms of birds, figures, animals, plants, cherubs and curlicues.

The earliest mirrors were made of highly polished metal. In the Gothic period, mirrors were often set in ivory frames and decorated with reliefs of chivalric subjects. As the manufacture of mirrors became more sophisticated, so did the frames surrounding them. In the late 17th and 18th centuries, the most famous British maker of frames was Grinling Gibbons, whose work was characterized by delicate carved limewood festoons of accurately rendered leaves, fruit and flowers. These and other period examples may be useful as sources of inspiration: look at books, catalogues and postcards for possible ideas.

The ease with which papier mâché can be shaped makes it possible to produce frames in elaborate, naturalistic forms — perhaps a seething mass of intertwined figures and animals, assuming you have the necessary modelling skills. Alternatively, you could rely on texture and subdued colour to make the impact you are looking for.

The versatility of papier mâché will enable you to create whatever style of mirror or picture frame you desire. With experience, you may learn to imitate other framing materials — carved and gilded wood, decorative plaster work, or even, as illustrated here, richly patterned cloth.

You can either work around an existing picture or mirror (which will give you the best fit), or you can make the frame separately and then add the picture or mirror. Both pulped paper and the layering method can be used to construct a frame. To protect the artwork or glass while you apply the papier mâché, cover it with a thin sheet of paper secured with tape.

You can have a mirror cut to any size or shape you wish or alternatively you can purchase mirror tiles and mount them onto lino, cork or cardboard. You can create wonderful works of papier mâché art by recycling worthless old mirrors with partially

How to make a frame

Equipment and materials	Paper for papier mâché
	Blank paper — for
Newspaper	example, typing paper
Mirror	Pen for drawing design
Chicken wire	Gouache paints
Paper to cover mirror	Paint brushes
Masking tape	Coloured pencils
Milliner's, florist's or	Emulsion paint
other flexible wire	Matt polyurethane
Jeweller's hammer	varnish
Wallpaper paste	Sharp craft knife

1 *Protect your working surface with a thick layer of newspaper. Place the mirror or picture alongside a length of chicken wire. To protect the glass or artwork while you work, cover with a thin piece of paper; tape securely in place. Bend the ends of the chicken wire over so that the mirror or picture is cradled all around (a).*

2 *If you wish to add an embellishment to the frame, form this out of a separate piece of chicken wire. Manipulate or hammer the wire with a small jeweller's hammer until you are satisfied with the shape (b). Start again with a new piece if things go wrong.*

3 *Add any such embellishments, using milliner's, florist's, or any other flexible wire (c); twist the ends of the wire together to hold the shape in place.*

4 *Mix up the wallpaper paste according to the manufacturer's instructions. Tear the paper into strips; dip the strips into the paste and apply the first layer of paper to the frame all around (d). Also cover the edges of the mirror or picture and any shapes that have been added to the frame. Allow to dry thoroughly.*

5 *When the first layer of glue and paper is dry, add the second and third layers, positioning the strips of paper*

removed silver or by using inexpensive mirrors with plastic frames. The original shape of the mirror need not necessarily dictate the shape of the final object, because the edges may be extended with papier mâché, or the mirror itself may be partially covered.

As with all papier mâché, your frame will need to be protected once the work is complete. Varnishing is especially important if your mirror is going to grace a humid room such as a bathroom or sauna!

Animation and wit are the hallmarks of these two mirror frames, both made from layered papier mâché on a chicken wire frame. The top one is inspired by antiquity, with two columns supporting vases, each containing a plant. The curtain blowing in the wind creates an opportunity for rich pattern. The bottom mirror contains small individual mirrors within a large furled frame. (Jennie Neame)

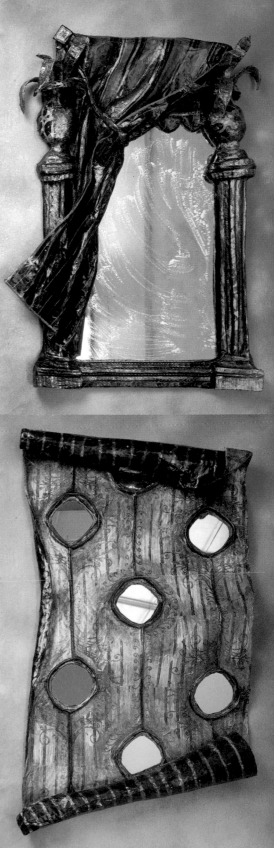

in opposite directions for each layer. Allow to dry thoroughly between each layer.

6 If you wish to create a printed draped cloth effect, draw a design in pen onto a piece of typing paper. Trace or photocopy the design several times. Paint the design with the colours of your choice. Tear the painted paper into strips (e) and layer it onto the frame in the area that is to resemble drapery. Paint the rest of the papier mâché frame with emulsion paint in the desired colour.

7 After the painted paper has dried onto the papier mâché, touch up any areas that need highlighting or toning down, using a coloured pencil or a fine paint brush and gouache paint (f).

8 When the frame is completely dry, paint it with a coat of matt polyurethane varnish.

9 Using a sharp craft knife, carefully cut away the paper covering the mirror or picture as close to the edge of the papier mâché as possible.

Wall plaques offer plenty of opportunities for sculptural inventiveness. Basic modelling skills are needed, but beginners who start on simple shapes will soon find their abilities and confidence growing — in step with their ambitions.

Plaques

Essentially flat-backed objects designed to hang against a wall, plaques often resemble masks, but without the holes for eyes and mouth. However, plaques need not take a figurative form: they can represent a wide range of imagery, including emblematic animals, birds, fish, plants or flowers, or they can take abstract or semi-abstract form.

Plaques lend themselves to casting in moulds, but for a more individual approach you might prefer to make them by hand, using pulp on an armature.

A single small plaque on a wall often looks somewhat forlorn: try making a series of pieces, perhaps resembling each other but with significant variations of form or decoration to prevent monotony.

The secret of success with plaques is to ensure that they can be "read" from a distance — that is, that their form is instantly recognizable, even in silhouette. This is the reason that simple ideas tend to work best — a human bust, a bird in flight, a palm tree, a 1920s car. This does not preclude, however, intricacy and inventiveness in the details and decoration of the piece.

Allowing the outline to make a graphic shape against the wall is one approach. Another is to enclose the plaque within a frame, as shown opposite.

Left: Wall plaques can be transformed into candle holders. This example, evoking the goddess of the moon, was constructed from pulped papier mâché built up over an armature. After the pulp was dry, it was sanded, then painted gold before being sanded again. (Louise Vergette)

Right: This exuberant piece of work, made in layered papier mâché, is a formalized picture contained within an intricate frame which itself becomes part of the piece. Two figures — a man and a woman — flank a vase of flowers. The colours are bright and pure, the imagery strong and carried out with great conviction. (Deborah Schneebeli-Morrell)

The armature technique enables you to make a plaque of relatively complex shape, perhaps even with over-lapping or intertwined elements. For more simple forms you might prefer to make a special mould, so that you can repeat the design.

The instructions here refer to making a wall plaque by the pulp method, using an armature that incorporates both wood and wire in its construction — the wood to provide the basic frame, the wire to support the intricate parts of the plaque.

It is important not to rush the early prepara-tion. A preliminary sketch is essential. After drawing the basic form you should draw in the skeleton, following every branch of the plaque's shape.

How to make a plaque

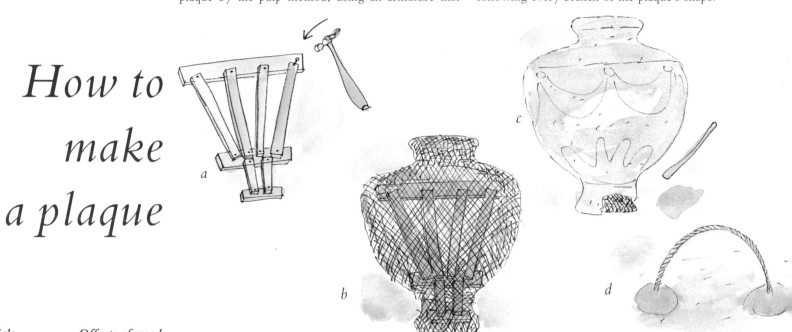

Equipment and materials

Newspaper
Large jam-making
pancheon/saucepan
Wooden spoon
Strainer
Sawdust: same quantity
as pulp
White glue: 2 cups
Whiting/ground chalk:
half the quantity of pulp
Linseed oil: 2 tablespoons
Oil of cloves: a few drops
Wallpaper (wheat) paste

Offcuts of wood
Nails and hammer, or
screws and screwdriver
Small-gauge chicken wire
Tin snips/wire cutters
Flat-nosed pliers
Small jeweller's hammer
Sculpting tools
Sandpaper
Sturdy wire
Emulsion paint
Materials for decorating
Paintbrushes
Matt polyurethane
varnish

1 *See the instructions for making pulp, pages 26-7. Rip the newspaper into small pieces and place in the large jam-making pancheon/saucepan, filling to the brim. Cover with water and boil the mixture for about three hours until the paper becomes pulp.*

2 *Strain off the surplus water and add the sawdust, white glue, ground chalk, linseed oil, oil of cloves and wallpaper (wheat) paste. Mix together.*

3 *Construct a simple wooden armature (a): this need only be the width and length of the finished piece, as the details can be created with the chicken wire.*

4 *Cut a piece of chicken wire to the approximate size you require. Using flat-nosed pliers, bend the chicken*

wire around the armature, creating a more detailed form upon which you can place the pulp (b). Use a small jeweller's hammer and the pliers to manipulate the wire.

5 *Next apply the pulp to the wood and chicken wire armature, front and back. The pulp will feel like clay. Using your hands and assorted pottery tools, shape and manipulate the pulp onto and around the chicken wire (c).*

6 *Allow the plaque to dry thoroughly; this can take up to three weeks. As the plaque dries, keep re-working the pulp to prevent any distortion or cracking.*

7 *Use the pliers to form a hanging loop from sturdy wire. Embed the loop in the pulp on the back of the plaque, covering the ends with additional pulp (d).*

The wire loop for hanging can easily be embedded into the pulp before it is dry. Alternatively you could simply fashion a small, lipped hole at the back to hang over a nail.

After the plaque has dried, the shape you have is unlikely to be exactly as you want it, but the advantage of pulp is that its form can easily be refined by sanding.

8 When the plaque is completely dry, sand the surface with sandpaper (e).

9 To seal and prepare the surface for further decoration, paint with white or black emulsion paint, depending on whether you want the plaque to have a light or dark finish. Allow the paint to dry thoroughly.

10 Add your final decorations. If you wish to apply foil paper, whether smooth or crumpled for texture, attach it to the paper mâché with white glue (f).

11 When your plaque is finished and thoroughly dry, apply a coat of clear matt polyurethane varnish.

The urn wall plaque here was made by Louise Vergette, using pulp made to a historic recipe. Although this artist's finishes are rich in appearance, they are produced inexpensively — for example, she uses foil from candy wrappers to produce a gold finish. (Louise Vergette)

Papier mâché can be used to decorative purpose in something every household needs — lampshades. When light is transmitted through paper, the effects can be beautiful. But be sure to follow the safety rules given below.

Lights

Right: This lampshade, constructed on the collage principle, so that the construction becomes part of the decoration, produces a subtle quality of illumination. The light transmitted gives the handmade paper a feeling of mellow warmth and highlights those areas that have fewer layers. The glow is enhanced by small pieces of silk that were added at the final stage, before the outside of the lampshade was varnished. (Maureen Hamilton-Hill)
Left: Symbolism informs this unusual table light made using paper pulp: the woman represents fertility, while the fish is an emblem of life. The modelling and detail are very fine. (Louise Vergette)

The qualities of translucency and lightness make papier mâché an obvious medium for lampshades, and the medium's versatility and strength make it suitable for lamp bases as well.

Traditional-style lampshades are usually supported on a wire frame that holds the shade away from the bulb. Such frames can make useful, if scanty, armatures but are not essential to the imaginative papier mâché artist. Any kind of framework, bought or devised, will do, provided that it is robust and firm.

The translucency of paper can be used to great effect in papier mâché lampshades. Variegated textures and colours, as found in handmade paper, enhance the effect. By varying the amount and thickness of paper you can control the quality and quantity of transmitted light. Further decoration can turn your lamp into a scintillating jewel.

Safety, of course, is paramount. Always apply a fire retardant in the final stages of making the lamp; and be sure to use a low-wattage bulb.

You can make a lamp base by passing a wire down a sturdy tube of cardboard, such as those used for rolls of fabric or carpeting. Secure the tube to a weighted base to prevent it from toppling. When you cover the tube with papier mâché (layers or pulp), remember to leave a hole for the wire. Fit the top of the base to an ordinary lamp fixture, which will hold the shade.

Of course, you need not restrict yourself to classical shapes. Using basic modelling skills you can make figurative bases. Or following the armature method you can produce lamps that are integral with their shades. You might even like to try making a multiple lamp — perhaps a scattering of fairy lights on a curvaceous (even a figurative!) stand built over an armature. The superb fish lamp opposite shows what can be achieved with skill and imagination.

You can work on a giant scale in papier mâché. To add distinction to an interior, screens and columns can be created, evoking whatever decorative style appeals to you. Trompe l'oeil effects can be integrated into designs, or you can opt for subtle, abstract decoration that is enhanced by the texture.

Screens

AND COLUMNS

Screens offer an opportunity for a striking design statement. This unusual example is made by layering on a chicken wire network, wound around a wooden frame. The first two panels are draped with a large papier mâché curtain and tieback, the third section has an inbuilt plinth with urn, while the last section includes an ornately decorated mirror frame. The piece is hinged and functions in the same way as a conventional screen. (Jennie Neame)

In the past, papier mâché was used extensively for the manufacture of architectural mouldings, wall brackets, and various kinds of ornamental detailing, as well as wall partitions in buildings, boats and trains. With the recent revival of papier mâché as a craft, it is not surprising that architectural forms are now being imitated in the same medium. Some papier mâché artists are reinterpreting classical and traditional motifs in a modern idiom.

Paper screens, popular in Japan for many hundreds of years, have uses too in modern, Western interiors, where they provide the most flexible and decorative way to divide a living space. There are two basic design approaches. One is to concentrate on the qualities of the paper itself, producing an object enjoyable for its subtle understatement; the other is to use the screen as a vehicle for flamboyant decoration and inventive wit.

The column has enjoyed a tremendous revival as a motif: it appears, for example, in the design of textiles, greetings cards, murals and wrapping paper, perhaps reflecting a new popular interest in architecture. Freestanding columns in papier mâché can be used to display ceramics, or busts, or antiquities (real or reproduction) — or perhaps a vase of flowers. A mottled, marble-effect paint treatment is often the most effective decoration.

Papier mâché screens can take many decorative forms. Surfaces can be smooth or in high relief. Decoration can be muted or bold. And there are plenty of opportunities for illusionistic effects or visual jokes.

One of the key features of a screen is that its essential form usually remains simple — a series of hinged panels — however exuberant or complex the decoration. There is thus no difficulty in reconciling the decoration to the structure: you can give your imagination full rein, knowing that even the most extravagant design will be disciplined by the rectilinear framework, and that the basic function of the screen as a room-divider will not be compromised.

This does not mean that a screen cannot be given flamboyant decorative attachments. Screens built up around an armature support can be embellished by building the papier mâché outward. Or the framework itself, before its skin is added, can be covered with papier mâché and sculpted in a modern version of the Art Nouveau style.

For a refined look, conjuring up the aesthetic of Japan, it is worthwhile using high-quality, textured paper — ideally handmade — perhaps combined with understated hand decoration. The richer style of lacquered Oriental screens, popular in Europe during papier mâché's heyday in the 19th century, can also be imitated in the medium.

The column is the ultimate expression of classical design — an instantly recognizable symbol, evoking a sympathetic attitude to the past.

A good method of production is to use a cylinder of chicken wire on a circular wooden frame. After you have layered the bottom foot or so to its ultimate thickness, you can pour in some quick-drying cement to give the column stability, then proceed with the layering up to the top of the column.

When creating columns in papier mâché, it is up to you how closely you follow classical originals. The five major Orders or classical styles of architecture, categorized according to the style of the columns themselves and the surmounting "entablatures", provide a source of inspiration. If you want to accurately reproduce a column, the Doric Order is the least ornate, but it might be more interesting to copy the Ionic Order, which consists of a fluted column with a "capital" (upper part) of twin scrolls: the flutes and scrolls need not be modelled, but instead can be drawn in. More complex is the Corinthian Order, which has acanthus leaf motifs in the capital.

The straight lines and neutral colours of antique architecture cry out for trompe l'oeil additions — a swathe of papier mâché fabric, a cupid, climbing ivy, or a creeping insect.

Various historic themes inspired this amazing artefact. The basic column form stems from antiquity, although its decoration has William Morris overtones. The floral drapes have a 1950s feel. As with the rest of her work, the artist has added papier mâché to a chicken-wire frame, itself wound around a wooden structure that gives stability and strength. The last layer added to the column consisted of photocopies of a hand-drawn design: these were hand-coloured and then varnished. (Jennie Neame)

Three elegant screens, each eight feet (2.5m) high, convey a Japanese mood, thanks to stark imagery and an effective monochrome palette. Together they would make wonderful room dividers, or could even be placed in front of a window so that the sunlight would glow through them. They are made of layers of textured paper and glue. (Henny Burnett)

Furniture was often made of papier mâché in the 19th century but the fanciful, distinctive pieces shown here are a long way removed from their historic counterparts. Figurative or animal furniture works well in children's rooms, but can also make a striking impact elsewhere.

Furniture

Papier mâché enables you to create something original, beautiful or witty out of a useless or ugly object such as an old chair, table or bureau, at very little cost. Sculptural forms on chair arms or legs, or on table legs, can be added to old furniture by constructing a chicken wire armature over the basic framework. Of course, instead of working with existing furniture you can make your own simple constructions, for example using plywood and lengths of square-section wood for a table or stool.

If your papier mâché furniture is going to be functional, it is important that it is finished off properly. This means applying many coats of varnish, especially if the article is to be used outside.

The examples illustrated here have an element of fantasy in them, but you could equally well work in a more restrained style to create distinctive pieces for the living room. For example, you could add scrolls or other decorative mouldings to an old chair or table. Pseudo-Chinese decoration in gold on a black or red base would be historically authentic: old auction catalogues or antiques magazines should give you plenty of inspiration.

Clock cases offer a particularly rich field for experiment. To a basic wall clock you could add an elaborate "apron" to serve as a base for decoration. A shoe box or other wooden or cardboard box could be used as a basic frame, or you could make your own case using fundamental carpentry techniques.

Above: This table, constructed in mixed media, uses papier mâché on an armature for the legs. The top is plywood, decorated with black-grouted bits of broken glass. (Louise Vergette)

Right: Animal forms can give furniture a strong sense of personality. These works are dyed rather than painted, which gives a more realistic finish. (Norma Bottell)

FASHION

Not least of the qualities of papier mâché that make it ideal for jewelry is its lightness. Large, flamboyant pieces can be displayed without weighing down the wearer. Or you can make smaller, elegant adornments that will win admiration at even the most refined social occasions.

Jewels

FROM JUNK

Papier mâché jewelry can be representational, depicting hands, doves, dogs, alligators, cats, fish, flowers, and the like, or it may be purely abstract and geometric. The shapes you make may be turned into bracelets, necklaces, pendants, earrings, hat pins, brooches, tie pins, buckles, shoe decorations or hair decorations. Buy jewelry attachments at bead shops or good haberdashery/notions departments and secure them onto the papier mâché pieces using a suitable, strong adhesive.

Because it is such a flexible medium, papier mâché can be made to imitate many other materials such as wood, resin, stone, shells and metal. It may be used to embed semi-precious or plastic stones or to support chains, beads, sequins, and so on.

Being small, jewelry is relatively quick to make, and it is often worth having a production line going so that you can be making, constructing and painting different pieces on the same day.

Papier mâché jewelry doesn't have to be precisely shaped: you can use layers of paper with torn edges to give a spontaneous quality to the work. It is easier to tear with the grain of the paper, but if you wish to produce a more irregular pattern, tear across the grain. Pulp may be squeezed out of a piping bag and used to produce a raised pattern on a piece of work. Another way of texturing work is to comb through the pulp with a tool such as a fork or a comb, or roll the pulp into balls and stick these onto the piece.

Other shapes can be made by squeezing the pulp between thumb and forefinger to create a wavy effect.

For design inspiration, look at natural elements such as shells, insects, stones or even fossils. Take some plaster casts of shells and then use these to cast papier mâché shells to serve as earrings or brooches. Leaves and flowers may also be formed from papier mâché. Lacquer, gold leaf, gilding and antique varnishes come into their own in the decoration of papier mâché jewelry to give a sophisticated finish which belies its humble origins.

Pages 94-5: Looking like fossils or lumps of copper, these jewels are in fact made from pulped papier mâché built up on pieces of cardboard. The clay-like pulp has been manipulated sometimes with the fingers, at other times with fine potter's tools. The colours have been painted on, one on top of another, and the top colour sanded to reveal the shimmering layer underneath. (Madeleine Child)

Right: These brightly coloured pieces have immediate impact. The pieces were layered around bowls used as moulds; sections of papier mâché were then cut away from the moulds to produce curved shapes. The decoration was painted, using a very fine brush and designer's gouache and acrylic paint. Each piece was then fitted with a jewelry attachment. (Yanina Temple)

Pulped or layered paper can be used in moulds, and then cut to shape. Make beads by rolling balls of pulp and then piercing them with a skewer. You can use the smallest bits of papier mâché cut away from moulds or discarded projects to form pieces of jewelry.

Jewelry making is the perfect medium for turning household waste paper, such as foil, cellophane and candy wrappers, into a form of decoration. So many household items can be used for decorating jewelry, such as old buttons, beads, stickers, studs, shells, bits of plastic, fabric flowers, chains and ribbons. You can use the cardboard from cereal and washing powder boxes for cutting templates.

Your jewelry doesn't have to be flat; it can be embossed with bits of tissue paper, string, pasta or beans and seeds. You can form rosettes by wrapping glue-soaked paper in a spiral. Or you can make curved pieces by layering papers in a bowl, cutting shapes

How to make a bangle

Equipment and materials

*Cardboard or
cardboard tube
Scissors or craft knife
Plastic bottle or similar
container
Wallpaper paste
Bowl for mixing
Newspaper
Coloured tissue paper
(optional)
Green and black paint,
gold metallic antiquing
polish (optional)
Clear polyurethane
varnish*

1 *Either unpeel or cut the cardboard tube along its spiralling seam (a). If the cardboard is very thick, use a sharp pair of scissors or a craft knife to cut it.*

2 *Stretch the cut cardboard open, giving the tube a larger circumference, but not flattening it. Fit the cardboard around a plastic bottle or a container such as a thermos that is approximately the diameter of an adult arm.*

3 *Mix wallpaper paste according to the manufacturer's instructions. Remove the cardboard from the plastic arm substitute. Tear strips of paper into pieces approximately 1 inch/2cm wide. Dip the torn paper into*

the paste and press the first piece onto the cardboard, smoothing the paper neatly into position. Add the next piece of paper so that it slightly overlaps the first (b).

4 *When the cardboard has been completely covered with the first layer of paste-covered paper, allow it to dry thoroughly. When the paper is nearly but not quite dry, put the cardboard back on the plastic bottle so that it will retain its shape (c).*

5 *Add the next layer of paper as you did the first, laying the pieces in the direction opposite the first layer. Allow to dry thoroughly.*

from the curved piece, then piercing these shapes with a needle so they may be hung on earring attachments. You can also work by layering papier mâché over a clay base.

The bangle shown right is constructed from cardboard. You can use cardboard strips, or (as explained in the instructions below) the insides of rolls of toilet paper, or the cardboard tubes around which tin foil or kitchen paper towels are rolled.

A collection of sophisticated jewelry all decorated to create a slightly glittery effect, but without being gaudy. The relief on the earrings was made by arranging string in a spiral pattern and then covering with a thin layer of papier mâché, so that the shape remained clear. The brooch at the bottom has been wired and earring droplets added for extra interest. (Sheer Decadence)

6 *Add subsequent layers to the outside of the cardboard bangle only, so as not to reduce the inside circumference and make the bangle too small to wear (d). After you have applied five layers, allow the bangle to dry thoroughly. While it is drying, work out your decorative scheme on rough paper. Experiment with colour combinations.*

7 *Decorate the bangle when it is completely dry. You can make the decoration an integral part of the bangle's construction by adding a layer of tissue paper in tones of the same colour or different colours. Or you may wish to paint the bangle as shown in the photograph*

(right): first apply a coat of green paint, then after the paint dries, rub the bangle with a metallic gold antiquing polish. Next, paint the inside of the bangle to contrast with the outside. Finally, paint the edges in a dark colour to give a strong outline and to help define the shape (e). The use of contrasting or harmonizing hues will create quite different effects.

8 *After the tissue paper, or paint and polish, are dry, apply a coat of clear polyurethane varnish to seal and finish the bangle (f). Allow the bangle to dry thoroughly before wearing.*

Light and therefore comfortable to wear, papier mâché is suitable for making hats for festive or fashionable occasions, or for children to use in their games of dressing up. The addition of other materials enhance a design.

Hats

Left: Papier mâché hats are for special occasions. These examples were made from layered papier mâché, built onto a plastic or ceramic form. The paintwork is beautifully detailed. Many coats of varnish have made these hats strong and waterproof. (Yanina Temple)

Your approach to papier mâché hatmaking will greatly depend on the intended purpose of the hats. Obviously, if you are making for children or for a fancy dress party, you can allow your imagination full rein, indulging in bright colours and ingenious motifs, and perhaps applying modelling skills to create some sort of spectacular crowning glory. At another extreme, you can make hats as fashion items, in which case you might prefer to take a more subdued approach.

It is possible to imitate other materials — for example, you could achieve the impression of leopardskin by clever paintwork. Insetting with mirrors or paste jewelry can create a glittering effect. Another strategy is to impress a woven texture into the papier mâché, to produce a bonnet-like appearance. Metal foil can convey the idea of a helmet.

Left: More a helmet than a hat, this design recalls the "Flappers" of the 1920s, and might look good with a shimmery dress. The bold bands of decoration on the hat have been thoughtfully placed to create a pleasing effect. (Yanina Temple)

Pages 102-103: A wonderful and witty collection of hats. Protruding beasts, bright colours, relief decoration and pyrography (controlled burning) are brought into decorative play. (Kate Sheppard)

If you coat papier mâché with linseed oil and then bake it, the papier mâché will be impervious to water; this makes it a perfect medium for creating a functional hat.

Suitable ready-made moulds might include basins, woks, footballs — or, for a fez-shaped hat, perhaps a flowerpot. If you layer using white glue for strength, fewer layers of paper — say, four or five — will be required, so that the finished object can be extremely light and flexible.

Another approach, described below, is to use cardboard shapes which are cut and taped together before being layered. This method allows for great variety of shape. If your hat is designed with a flat round top you can use a plate as a template. To make a pointed hat, draw a circle, cut it in half, and then roll it to form a cone.

Peaks or brims can easily be made out of cardboard. The best way to attach them is to leave a

How to make a hat

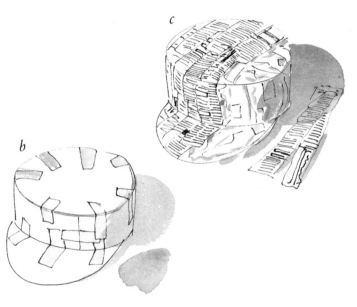

Equipment and materials

Pencil
Paper for sketching
Scissors
Adhesive tape or stapler and staples
Flexible cardboard
Craft knife
Wallpaper paste
Newspaper
Clear plastic wrap/saran wrap

Materials for decorating such as tissue paper, paints, bleach
Woodburning tool (optional)
Paintbrushes, various sizes
Matt polyurethane varnish

1 *Sketch the hat you would like to construct (a). Make up a pattern for your hat, cut out the pieces from thin paper, and join them together with tape. Try on the paper hat, adjusting until it fits.*

2 *Carefully take the paper pattern apart. Trace around each of the pieces to transfer the shapes to flexible cardboard, then cut out the cardboard using a craft knife. Join the pieces of the cardboard hat together using tape or staples (b). Trace, cut and join with care, for a good fit.*

3 *Mix up the wallpaper paste. Rip the newspaper into small pieces.*

4 *Cover the cardboard hat base with clear plastic wrap/ saran wrap. Dip the pieces of newspaper into the*

wallpaper paste and apply the first layer of paper to the plastic-covered hat base, overlapping the pieces as you go (c). Allow to dry thoroughly.

5 *Add the next layer of paper, placing the pieces in the opposite direction to the first layer. Allow to dry thoroughly. Add another five coats of paste-covered paper, drying thoroughly between layers.*

6 *Remove the cardboard base and the clear plastic wrap/saran wrap from the papier mâché.*

7 *To add three-dimensional surface decoration, dip bundles of tissue paper into the wallpaper paste and apply to the surface of the hat. When the tissue paper is dry, cover with another layer of paste-covered paper.*

narrow flap or series of flaps that you attach to the main body of the hat, folding it over on the inside. Then tape the flap(s) in place and cover the whole area with layers of paper and glue.

A fan-shaped concertina of paper makes an attractive embellishment for the front of a hat. Felt or other fabric can be used to cover the hat if you want a softer look, while a flamboyant, fun effect can be achieved using tassels or woollen bobbles.

Right: These three hats are variations on a theme — the application of papier mâché to a basic cardboard shape, and the use of pyrography (burning) to give blackened edges to cut patterns. The top hat has a hole cut and burnt in the top, and a fish beside the hole. The second hat has nodules and ledges and a stalk in the top. The bottom hat is peaked, with elaborate piercing. (Kate Sheppard)

8 *If you wish to add further interest to the design, use a craft knife to cut holes or other geometric shapes out of the papier mâché (d). Or paint a design on the hat.*

9 *Alternatively, you can cover the final layer of newspaper with overlapping pieces of different colour tissue paper, building up dense colour in some areas. If you wish to bleach out areas of colour on the tissue paper, dip an old paintbrush or piece of cloth into household bleach, and brush or rub the tissue paper after it is dry.*

10 *If you wish to decorate the hat by pyrography (burning), you will need a woodburning tool. Sketch the areas that you wish to burn directly on the hat. Depending upon the size of the area you wish to burn,* affix a fine, medium or coarse point onto the woodburning tool. Plug in the tool and allow the point to heat up. Test the tool on a spare piece of papier mâché; the point should not set the work alight. Carefully and lightly go over the lines you have drawn with the point of the woodburning tool (e). Or, cut out a hole and then burn the edges.

11 *When you are satisfied with the hat, coat the entire object, both inside and out, with matt polyurethane varnish (f). Be sure to allow the varnish to dry thoroughly before wearing the hat.*

MASKS AND DOLLS

These masks, which are one and a half times normal head size, are inspired by those made in Basel, Switzerland, for the carnival there. Their wistful, childlike quality makes them instantly appealing: they have mystery but not a trace of the grotesque. To make the masks, clay forms were modelled, then two-part moulds were made on them using plaster of Paris. The artist then pressed pulp into the moulds — a mixture of pulverized newspaper, fine sawdust, cellulose filler/spackle or gesso powder, and resin used as a glue. Fabric such as buckram (used for stiffening belts), hessian, muslin/calico, or even leather, was used to provide a backing for the finished masks, and to make them durable, and comfortable to wear. The drying time was about one week. They were then rubbed down, gessoed and rubbed down again to remove all traces of coarseness. The worn look of the masks is part of their appeal. (Jeff Higley)

Throughout history both adults and children have been fascinated by the idea of disguise — hence, the popularity of carnivals and masked balls. A mask is a potent, universal symbol.

Masks

The human face is the most powerful of all forms that can be represented artistically, and even the most minimal of features can convey a strong impression of personality. The masks here (left) show how abandonment of strict realism need not result in the grotesque but can lead to something much more benevolent, with mystery but not terror. The archaic feel of these masks relates to ancient feelings buried deep in our consciousness. These are not character masks, but they do show how an impression of human or superhuman force can be created by bold modelling.

The ribbons on one of the examples here provide perhaps the simplest way to attach a mask to the head: it is easy to make a pair of holes in the papier mâché after it has been formed. You could also use two elastic bands, one for each ear, but the ribbons are a more classic touch.

To make a mask comfortable to wear you might consider lining the edges with leftovers of felt or another soft fabric.

Pages 106-107: These three heads — a goat or camel, a rooster, and a frog — were inspired partly by Aesop's fables and partly by African tribal art. The heads were made on moulds of carved plastic foam. To remove them from their moulds they were cut and rejoined. The strong colours combine with the bold shapes to make an immediate impact. (Mike Chase)

How to make a carnival mask

A mask enables the wearer to take on an entirely new persona — a beast, a skeleton, a beautiful princess, a famous politician. Carnivals are a time for the wholesale exchange of identity.

The lightness of papier mâché makes it suitable for gigantic heads and bodies which tower above the people who wear them. Inspiration might come from a museum of ethnography, as most ancient cultures used masks. Cartoon strips might also provide ideas. Accessories such as whiskers or cardboard horns can help make the effect more impressive. Instead of wearing masks you can, of course, use them as wall decorations.

The instructions below describe the creation of a mask using entire layers of newspaper coated in white glue and laminated onto a clay model. This method of taking a direct cast is one of the swiftest ways to make a hollow mask. You will need a large

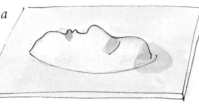

Equipment and materials

Large flat work surface
Modelling clay
Sculpting or pottery tools
Clear plastic wrap/saran wrap
Releasing agent — for example, petroleum jelly or oil
White glue
Water
Newspaper
Craft knife

Strong glue
Embellishments — for example, plastic animals, lizards, fish and the like
Materials for decorating such as glitter, seeds, string, paint or decorative paper
Elastic for securing mask to head
Matt polyurethane varnish
Brush

1 On a flat work surface, sculpt a mask out of modelling clay; do not make it too finely detailed or the details will be lost (a). When you are satisfied with the mask, cover the clay with clear plastic wrap/saran wrap to prevent it from drying out, then cover the plastic wrap/saran wrap with a releasing agent such as petroleum jelly or oil. Follow the contours of the mask closely with the wrap, so that the features will be reproduced in papier mâché.

2 Make a half-and-half mixture of glue and water. Spread a piece of newspaper flat on your work surface and coat it with the water/glue mixture. The paper will become very soggy.

3 You must work quickly as the glue will dry rapidly. Cover the clay mask with the paper, which will be very soft and spongy. One sheet of newspaper, torn into workable pieces, should easily cover the complete mask. You should have no difficulty working the paper into the details of your mask (b). When the paper starts drying, stop working it.

4 Allow the paper to dry overnight. Repeat the process with another coat of glued paper the next day. Allow this to dry thoroughly before applying a third layer in the same manner. You will not need many layers because the white glue will give a strong finish.

work surface, as the method can be quite messy, and all your materials readily to hand.

There are other ways to make a mask. One is to create a chicken wire armature on which to add layers of paper or pulp. Alternatively you can layer or pulp onto a mould such as an inflated balloon. You can make two masks from one balloon by cutting the dried papier mâché in half lengthwise after you have removed it from the balloon.

A set of mercurial, mask-like wall decorations, suggesting fire, movement, life. Each mask was made by constructing an original in clay and then covering this mould with layers of paper, heavily impregnated with glue. After completion of the layering and the final drying stage, the masks were removed from the clay originals, pieces were cut out of them, and paint and texture added. (Billy Nicholas)

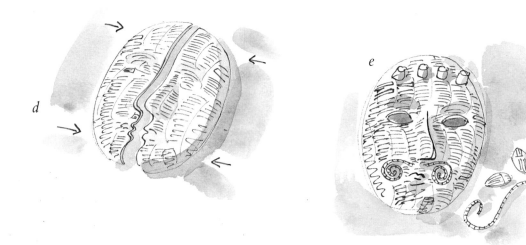

5 *When the final layer of paper is fully dry, remove the hard laminated shell from the mould. To do this, carefully cut the mask in half lengthwise using a sharp craft knife (c).*

6 *Join the two halves of the mask carefully together with strong glue (d).*

7 *Add any embellishments such as plastic animals, lizards, fish — anything your imagination can dream up. Make other three-dimensional embellishments either from glued paper twisted into shape or armatures covered with pulp. Decorate the mask with glitter, seeds, string, paint or decorative paper. If you plan to wear the*

mask, cut out eye holes and make a hole on each side for attaching elastic (e).

8 *When the mask is finished, apply a coat of matt polyurethane varnish, both inside and out.*

9 *If you intend to wear the mask but have sensitive skin, you can stick or stitch a layer of soft fabric to the finished inside surface, or at the points that come in close contact with your face. Fine felt, silk, satin or lightweight cotton would be suitable.*

Dolls are usually made as playthings, but can also take the form of exquisite craft objects purely for display. Made in historic styles, as shown opposite, they can vividly evoke a lost age of innocence.

Dolls AND PUPPETS

Left: Based on nursery rhyme nostlagia, these dolls look as if they were made in a bygone age. The heads and limbs are papier mâché, and the torsos stuffed silk and calico/muslin. Some of the dolls are jointed at the elbows and knees, while others are jointed only at the shoulders and the hips — by simple loops of cotton. The bodices are printed onto the calico, and the shoes, faces and hair painted on the papier mâché. This artist studied embroidery, and her dolls reflect her interest in this medium. (Melanie Williams)

Far right: Only the head of this puppet is papier mâché, but if you wish you can make the limbs and torso in this medium too. (Mike Chase)

Papier mâché can be the principal material in doll-making, or it can be used just for the head and limbs and combined with a fabric body — for example, stuffed calico/muslin.

You can aim to convey a bygone mood, based on Victorian precedents, with lace trimmings and other old scraps of fabrics, suitably worn or faded; or alternatively you can use modern fabric in bright colours and patterns for a contemporary look. Either way, attention to detail, without making the doll appear too complex, is the secret of success. Bear in mind the scale of the printed pattern; choose something small to enhance your doll. Obviously, basic needlework skills make dollmaking much easier.

Hinging the limbs at knees and elbows gives extra versatility, but is not essential; shoulder and hip joints are more important in flexible dolls. It is worth looking at historic dolls in museums for inspiration.

Faces can be painted in a variety of expressions, from anger and boredom to astonishment, but should not be overworked: the most minimal arrangement of dots or lines can be used to convey character.

Jointed dolls can be turned into puppets with the addition of strong threads and a jointed "control panel". However, you should remember that a puppet needs a certain amount of weight if it is to be manipulated successfully and not get tangled. Contrive weights in the head and limbs to make the puppet easier to operate.

The instructions below describe how to make a doll by layering over a simple home-made mould. The basic procedure is easy: more difficult is the detailing, which must be carefully done — and not *over*done — for a successful result.

Dressing the doll is of key importance. Small scraps of old fabric can be used in ingenious ways. Scale is on your side — even the tiniest piece of lace can do service for a richly embroidered bodice. Buttons can be used as large buckles, as in the examples on page 112. Another approach altogether, illustrated opposite, is to paint the costume directly onto the papier mâché body.

The hair is best painted on, perhaps with stray curls to evoke the early 19th century. You can improvise wigs out of fabric. Mohair (from the hair of the Angora goat) knotted to a skull cap of linen is easy to style; however, it is difficult to clean and may shred if combed. Such wigs should be pasted to the head with a water-soluble glue.

How to make a doll

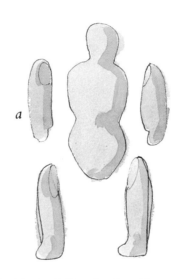

Materials and equipment

Plasticine/modelling clay
Releasing agent — such as petroleum jelly or oil
Newspaper
Wallpaper paste
Masking tape
Paint brushes
Varnish
Turpentine for washing brushes

1 *Soften the plasticine/modelling clay by taking a ball in your hands and manipulating it. Your body heat will make the material malleable. Fashion a combined torso and head shape in one, with just a slight indentation for the neck. Even a hat can become an extension of the head/body shape.*

2 *Now make the limbs by the same method. If you make each limb as a separate, unjointed item, there will be only four joints — at the shoulders and thighs (a). These can be quite sufficient.*

3 *Once the parts of the doll have been formed in this way, make sure that all the surfaces are smooth. Give each limb a good coating of releasing agent — for example, petroleum jelly or oil.*

4 *Rip up your newspaper into 1-inch (2.5cm) strips, dip each strip into the glue and wipe off any excess between your thumb and forefinger. Start layering evenly over the body and then the limbs (b). When each part has been covered with a layer of papier mâché, leave to dry before adding the next layer.*

5 *Repeat step 4 until you have built up half a dozen layers. When the papier mâché is dry, very carefully cut the paper shell off the body and off each limb using a scalpel or craft knife (c). If you wish to use the original model again, be careful not to cut too deeply or you will cut through the clay.*

6 *You will now have two pieces for each part of the doll. Stick each half to its other half using masking tape.*

Features should be highly stylized: any attempt at hyperrealism is bound to be unconvincing. Small blobs of red paint on the cheeks may seem a cliché but they do give strength to the features.

The details of hands and feet can be painted directly onto the limbs. Or you could paint on shoes and stockings, keeping them simple to avoid diverting too much attention from the more important parts of the doll — unless you are very adept with a paintbrush and can suggest laces or buckles convincingly.

These two dolls made by the layering method have a deliberately primitive quality about them — a suggestion of folk art conveyed by the bulky forms and bright colours. Although the forms are simple, the workmanship is meticulous. Note how the torso has been shaped at the base to accommodate the upper parts of the legs. (Deborah Schneebeli-Morrell)

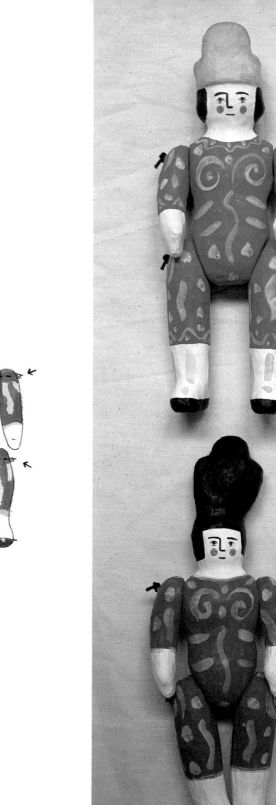

Add three more layers of papier mâché to cover the joint, drying between each layer.

7 When the final layer of paper mâché is dry, paint the body and limbs in white poster paint. This is a good base colour on which to work. However you may prefer a dark doll with a gold or another metallic finish, in which case use black or dark blue as a base coat. Leave to dry.

8 Paint on the facial features, the hands and feet or shoes, and any patterns on the body (d). You may wish to paint on clothes, if you are not making clothes to fit on the doll.

9 When the paint is dry, the limbs may be attached to the torso. This may be done using the special fixtures for doll and teddy bear making: these may be bought in good craft shops and haberdashery/notions departments.

10 As an alternative method, pierce holes in the top of each limb and on the torso where the limbs are to be attached, using a darning needle. Push shirring elastic through the limbs and torso holes together, knotting each end of the elastic, which must be fairly tight but still allow the limbs to move (e). Cover the knot, if you wish, with more papier mâché. Retouch the paintwork if necessary.

11 When the retouched paint is dry, protect the doll with a coat of clear varnish.

Most people do not associate papier mâché with fine art. However, many artists use papier mâché, or related forms of pulping and layering, to produce art objects as subtle in their impact as anything worked on canvas.

Art

Pages 116-117: This piece of abstract art is made from papier mâché pulp and other materials such as wood and yarn. The paper, after being pulped, was dyed to the required colours. Then the work was built up on a mesh of fabric to form an abstract pattern in relief. More colour was added as the work progressed. (Keith Roberts)

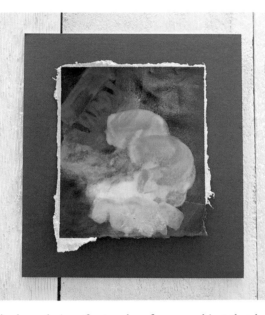

Left: These pieces were made by building up layers of pulped paper and glue on a sheet of bookbinder's mull. Some of the layers were mixed with calico/muslin or other fibres. The resulting sandwich of materials was pressed under weights for 24 hours, dried, and then manipulated by being torn, cut, painted, and then torn or cut again. (Brian Bishop)

The boundaries of art and craft are a subject that has provoked some vigorous debate: where does one end and the other begin? It is not the purpose of this book to enter the fray, but simply to hint at the whole range of possibilities in papier mâché, without worrying overmuch about nomenclature.

In devoting a section to art objects, the aim is not to draw a frontier. Many of the other objects shown in this book — for example, the Indian-inspired work of Katherine Virgils (pages 46-7) — undoubtedly qualify as fine art. The intention over the following pages is simply to gather together in one place a number of highly imaginative works to indicate the rich potential of the medium.

Increasingly, artists experienced in other media are turning to paper for self-expression. This partly reflects an interest in using recycled materials; as one artist, Theodora Fandousi, has put it, paper pulp "recycles matter that would otherwise be discarded, and provides a strong, natural binding medium".

Right: A work of pure abstraction formed using pulped computer paper dyed with various analine dyes and then placed on a mesh of fabric and impressed with an irregular, swirling pattern. The contrasting light and shaded areas give a cool acidity to this piece. (Keith Roberts)

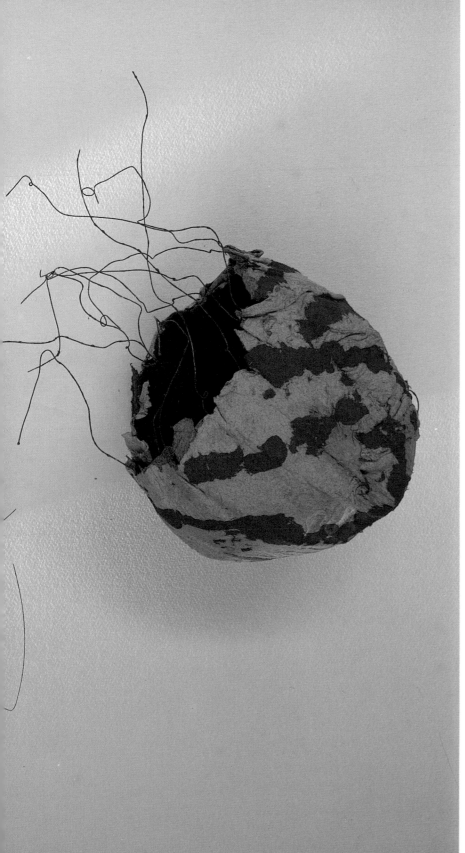

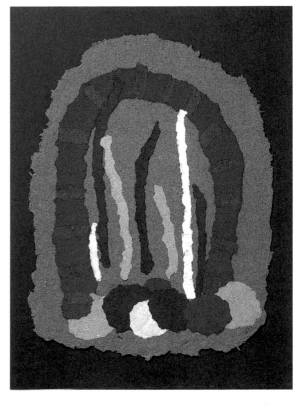

Right: The work of Henny Burnett, shown on these pages, is inspired by aspects of cities — subways, architecture, graffiti, and the repetitive patterns and shapes we find in the urban environment. She works in handmade papers, building up layer upon layer. These two collages within frames show the delicacy of effects she achieves, and contrast dramatically with her sculptural work. (Henny Burnett)

Left: Pod-like in appearance, these pieces of sculpture are built up of thick layers of handmade paper wrapped around one another. Wires running through the forms help to maintain their shape. The rich, dense colours are a hallmark of this artist. (Henny Burnett)

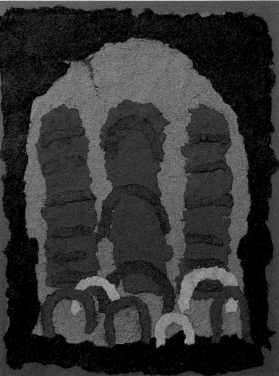

Left: This work by Alison Lockhead evokes an arid landscape. It incorporates pulp made from plant fibres. The artist comments: "For the images I am trying to create, paper pulp has the spontaneity, the crispness and the variety of texture that I need, along with the flexibility to add further images by drawing or painting onto the piece." (Alison Lockhead)

Right: This piece was made in a similar way to its companion on these pages, but the world evoked is cooler, wetter, more flowing. The shape on the left, terracotta in hue, looks like a dry peninsula in a sea subtly graded with colours. (Alison Lockhead)

Handmade and pulped papers can reveal an infinity of textural and sculptural qualities, as evidenced by these two pieces based mainly on responses to the colours, textures and forms of the landscape.

Different materials and techniques may be used to capture the various moods and the manifold forms of nature, such as dry, dusty plains, soft, waving leaves, hot, steamy jungles.

In such pieces there is scope for a direct affinity between the medium and what the medium represents, as the papers can be made from straw, bracken, grass, nettles or bamboo leaves which are boiled in caustic soda/lye to break down the hard outer fibres and release the inner fibres. The plants are then washed thoroughly and dyed before being pulped in a blender. The sheets are then made on a special meshed frame known as a "mould and deckle": refer to a book on paper making for precise instructions.

Many plants can be used for making paper, each producing a different texture. The textures can also be varied by the fineness or coarseness with which the plants are cut up, as well as by the length of time for which they are blended. To some extent there is an element of chance involved here: the results are not precisely predictable. However, this is all part of the challenge and interest of producing art from handmade paper, and you may be delighted with the unexpected effects. Experiment to find your ideal recipe.

The mixture of paper with other media, following instinctive rather than preconceived lines of approach, can produce stunning effects, as shown in the examples opposite, by Theodora Fandousi.

This artist creates both pots and free compositions, and there is much cross-fertilization of ideas between the two media. The compositions are constructed in shallow relief and are designed as wall hangings. A crooked frame is built around each piece, and this becomes part of the work. The visual imagery of these works consists of naked and voluptuous human forms engaged in symbolic and mysterious activities in the company of various animals.

The artist says of her work: "Both the paintings and pots are made intuitively. Everything I have learned about the materials disappears from consciousness and my actions are led by instinct. Each piece grows out of an organic process, manipulated in an almost blind fashion until an identity emerges."

These pieces, unconstrained by conventional frames, are dynamic and vibrant. The artist describes her typical method thus: "Branches, twigs, leaves and seaweed are collected from outdoors. These organic materials are combined with scrap paper, which is pulped, sometimes to a semi-fluid consistency. Sometimes the paper is simply torn and then tied or pasted onto the wooden framework." (Theodora Fandousi)

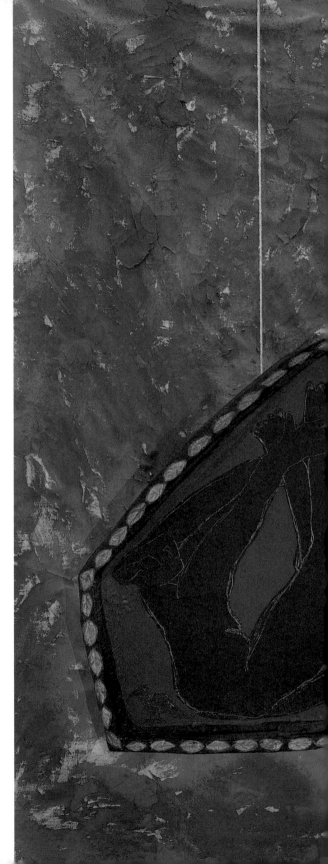

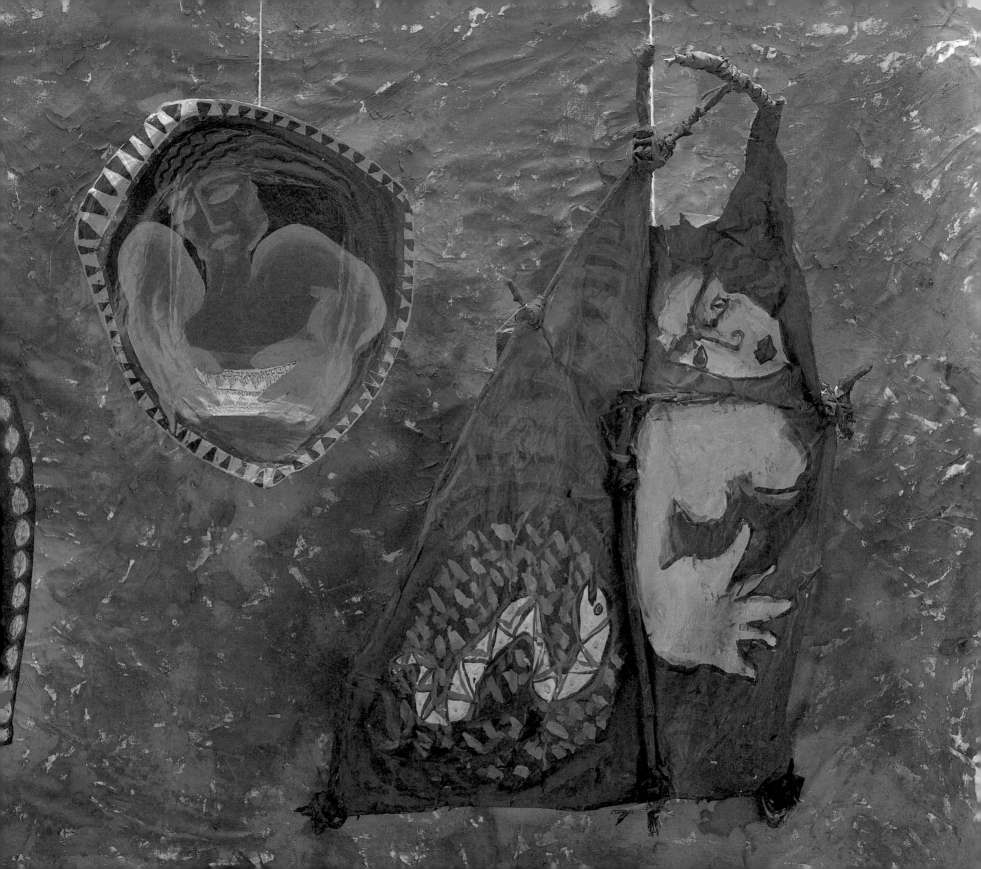

The difficulty of working traditional materials, and the special equipment necessary, deter many talented people from trying their skills on sculpture. Papier mâché provides a way out of this frustration.

Sculpture

The absence of rules in sculpture, the freedom to explore and experiment, make it an exciting art form indeed. To produce a work of sculpture is to collaborate with your material in an alliance of mind and matter, with matter the dominant partner.

Paper used sculpturally may seem to be something of a paradox. Julia Manheim, the artist whose work is shown on these pages, puts it as follows: "There is a kind of magic in creating an object which is structurally strong, with a powerful personality, from such a flimsy material as newspaper."

It is worth remembering that even the most adventurous experiments need to be performed with discipline. Thorough planning is essential, and careful construction is needed at every stage, from the creation of the armature to the final decoration.

Left: Monumentality and precision are the hallmarks of the pieces on these pages. **Inflationary Spiral** *(left) is 4 feet (126cm) in diameter. Shaped like an ammonite, it is made of cardboard boxes, which is why it has a beautifully undulating appearance. (Julia Manheim)*

Right: This boat and bird are about 2½ feet (75cm) long. They are made of layered newspaper and glue built around an exact cardboard armature. Neither form nor decoration is predominant, but both of these elements are held in perfect balance. (Julia Manheim)

Although these papier mâché figures are based on real people, they are composites, each one drawing on the characteristics of more than one individual. For construction, the artist has used the unusual technique of gradually building up a structure of cardboard and paper. No painting was involved: all the colour and pattern is provided by the scrap paper that the figures incorporate. The artist usually begins a piece by working on the face: this often determines the direction in which the stance or outline of the body will progress. Many pieces never move further than the head and torso, as they are often found to be complete at this stage. (Philip Cox)

Quirkily extrovert, the figures here all show a highly inventive use of the medium. All the figures were made entirely from waste paper and cardboard, without any supporting framework. The paper used was chosen for its colour: even the skin is made of paper of an appropriate hue. The kneeling woman (above right) is the epitome of the English cleaning lady, the strain on her face, the overplucked eyebrows and the large coarse hands all helping to create realism. The three men (right) are a wonderful piece of observation on the part of the artist — the way they hold themselves, the hang of their clothes, make it hard not to see them

as real people. The couple staggering out of an English public house (above left), although still based in reality, are more a satiric comment on human weakness than a lifelike sculpture.

When planning a figurative sculpture in papier mâché, it helps to have a miscellany of photographs and sketches to work from: you will need views from all angles, including the back. Ask friends to model or take shots of unsuspecting strangers. If you are going to make the surface decoration an integral part of the construction, you will need to collect a vast array of coloured and textured papers and fabrics.

A papier mâché figure — whether free-standing or a wall plaque — may have an expression unique to him or her, or an exaggerated expression that derives from a recognizable human type.

For life-size sculptures, you will need a large room for working and for storing the materials that you have collected for your constructions. It is worth accumulating household waste paper such as paper bags, cardboard boxes and cylinders of all sizes, as well as a large supply of newspapers.

Hair can be made from yarn or tissue dipped in glue. Start at the bottom of the head and apply the yarn or tissue in layers, working upward. Trim the finished "hair" with scissors to obtain the right shape or cut. Drapery can be formed from large sheets of paper dipped in glue, or fabric dipped in glue and treated in the same way as papier mâché. Cheesecloth, muslin, lace and other fine fabrics all drape well when

How to make a figure

Equipment and materials

Newspaper
Cardboard boxes of all sizes and shapes, paper bags, cardboard cylinders
Waste paper
Masking tape or brown gummed tape
Staple gun and staples
Craft knife
Wallpaper (wheat) paste
Paper and fabric in a

variety of patterns and textures for the clothing or skin
Yarn or tissue paper for hair
Emulsion paint and any other paints or dyes required for decoration
Paintbrushes
Clear polyurethane varnish

1 *Make sketches or take photographs from all angles of the figure you wish to create. Then study your drawings or photographs and imagine your figure stripped of all its flesh and clothing. The shape you are visualizing is the skeleton which you must construct.*

2 *Examine your cardboard boxes, cylinders and papers to find the pieces that most closely replicate the basic shapes of your skeleton. For example, use cardboard cylinders for arms or legs, a rectangular cardboard box for the torso and a square cardboard box for the head, compressed at one end to resemble a neck (a).*

3 *Join all your body pieces together using masking tape, brown gummed tape and/or a staple gun (b).*

4 *After all the body parts are attached, study the skeleton critically to see if any areas need adjusting. You may need to bulk out a joint between an arm and the body, or fill out a face that appears too flat. To bulk out these areas, crumple paper bags, tissue paper or newspaper, dip the crumpled paper into wallpaper (wheat) paste, then stick in place onto your skeleton. Do not overdo this: your final figure may look overstuffed. It is better to produce the finer details through the application of papier mâché.*

5 *When you are satisfied with your skeleton, begin applying layers of paper following the directions for layered papier mâché (see pages 36-7). Dip strips of paper into the wallpaper (wheat) paste and smooth onto your*

first dipped in glue. You could also use fabric with a small-scale print as the final layer of your papier mâché — an effective, convincing touch.

You can use an armature or skeleton to make a figure, as described in the instructions below. Alternatively, you could use a purely cumulative method, which is more unusual. This is appropriate if you want to achieve an expressive result, rather than a meticulously realistic one.

Character can often be captured just as well in a head-and-shoulders wall plaque as in a full-length figure. The three highly animated life-size busts here show people absorbed in characteristic actions. The man at the top is taking snuff, the lady in the middle applying her lipstick, the woman at the bottom knitting. The skilful modelling is especially apparent in the hands, which are full of movement. (Philip Cox)

skeleton, overlapping each strip slightly. Continue until the skeleton is covered with the first layer of paper (c). Allow to dry thoroughly.

6 Continue applying layers of paper to build up the shape of your figure. You will need to apply a minimum of four layers, but keep adding layers until your figure is completely "fleshed out." Concentrate on the face, adding small bits of paper to create the facial expression you wish to achieve. Apply short strips of flesh-coloured tissue paper as your last layer of skin (d).

7 When the figure's body is the size and shape you desire, you can begin adding the clothes. Use patterned papers or fabrics for a dress, shirt or tie (e). Select papers or fabrics in the colours and textures that most resemble the kind of clothing you want your figure to be wearing. For added authenticity, add real buttons, tie tacks or other decorative items to the clothing using some paste to secure them firmly.

8 When the final layer of clothing is thoroughly dry, coat your entire figure with clear polyurethane varnish Allow the varnish to dry thoroughly.

When making beasts in papier mâché you can strive for a form of heightened realism, or if you prefer you can evolve your own creatures, otherworldly or weird, perhaps to adorn a playroom or child's bedroom — or modified to make unusual lamps or frames.

Strange

BEASTS

Myths, common to all cultures, often feature animals in the role of evil, with a man as the heroic protagonist. There is also, of course, a benign side: animals can symbolize power, instinct, luck, or plenty. Pick your culture, and select your magical creature.

There are many possible sources of inspiration, ranging from children's book illustrations, to the carved animals in Gothic cathedrals, to the creatures of science fiction movies such as *Star Wars*.

Features such as teeth or claws often look most effective if made separately and inserted or otherwise attached. Avoid making the stance of the animal too symmetrical or it will look stiffly unrealistic. A flexed tail can help to impart a sense of life.

On a relatively small scale, animal forms could be incorporated into a mobile — in which case it would obviously be most appropriate to make flying creatures such as bats, birds or winged insects. Wings could be added using fabric stretched over a wire frame, or otherwise stiffened.

As a project for the playroom you could try making a whole zoo or Noah's ark, or perhaps a toy box in animal form. Imitation fur, or velvet, could serve as the pelt; more flamboyant fabrics could enhance a fantastical beast.

*Left: A wild, fearsome blue-green dog with raving eyes. The dog, known as **Mescalito** (after the drug mescalin), is constructed from pulped paper added to a wood and wire armature. A mixture of paints creates the strange blue glow. The texture of the piece has been left rough to suggest animal fur. The eyes are beads and the teeth are made of clay. (Louise Vergette)*

Left: Two alien creatures silently commune. They were built around a mould made in sculpted plasticine/modelling clay, to which sheets of PVA-soaked paper were added. After the main body of each figure was cut off the mould in two halves, then joined up again, an incredible wealth of detail was added — seeds, bits of postcard, fur, and many other decorative trimmings. Each piece was then carefully painted. (Billy Nicholas)

Right: This work, framed in wood, was designed to fit into the end of a church pew to remind parishioners of their lapses from grace: it belongs to a whole sequence depicting the Seven Deadly Sins. The piece consists of details in cardboard to which papier mâché was added — either as pulp, or as strips, or both. The pulp used was a fairly stiff mixture of torn-up newspaper, white glue and water, employed in much the same way as modelling clay. (Kevin Brockbank)

Right: This bizarre sculpture is created from pulped paper built onto a chicken wire frame. The piece represents our journey through life — precarious, unsteady, fraught with difficulty. It is not without significance that the woman is clothed: this represents our sometimes incongruous attempts to protect ourselves through formality and disguises. The piece is approximately 4 feet (1.2m) high. (Louise Vergette)

Right: Made by the same construction method as the other sculpture on these pages (left), this piece similarly has symbolic overtones. The fish symbolizes the force of life itself, from which the woman is being created, her serene expression reflecting innocence, a complete absense of worldly expectation. Her silvery skin is emblematic too, suggesting the shining soul free of earthly taints. The figure stands about 3½ feet (1m) tall. (Louise Vergette)

GLOSSARY

Armature A basic framework or skeleton (often of wire or wood) to which papier mâché is added.

Bagging A decorative technique whereby patches of glaze or paint are removed using a bag – paper or plastic – dipped in turpentine.

Bole A clay, usually reddish-brown, used as a pigment.

Burnish A sheen caused by rubbing.

Butt-joint The joint between two pieces of paper that have been stuck immediately adjacent to each other on a surface, without any gap or overlap.

Carton-pierre A material resembling old-fashioned grey egg cartons.

Chicken wire Wire netting, usually with a hexagonal mesh, bought by length.

Crackling A deliberately cracked surface effect, suggestive of age. Achieved by using a water-based paint and an oil-based paint on the same object: these dry at different rates, causing a network of fine lines. A ready-made crackle varnish produces a similar effect as it dries.

Découpage A collage of random pieces of paper which may carry illustrations or other designs.

Distress To give a piece a worn, antique appearance.

Emulsion A paint with a milky consistency.

Gesso A material used as a ground for painting or gilding, providing a smooth or moulded surface.

Glaze A transparent liquid, clear or coloured with pure pigment, that may be used as a final decorative and protective layer on the surface of papier mâché.

Gouache Opaque watercolour paint. Paints sold as "poster paints" are usually a form of gouache.

Gypsum The main ingredient in plaster of Paris.

Japan ware Any product made by japanning.

Japanning The term given to a method of imitating Oriental lacquer ware.

Lacquer A liquid that dries to a hard glossy finish, usually black or red.

Laminating Bonding together two or more sheets of material for extra thickness.

Layering A method of making papier mâché objects by building up layers of paper and glue. Each layer is allowed to dry before the next layer is added.

Lino cut A form of block printing which developed from the woodcut, but with linoleum used instead of wood to form the reusable block.

Linseed oil Oil from the seeds of flax. Used to extend the life of pulp, preventing the formation of mould; and, when baked, to waterproof an object.

Maquette A preliminary model for a sculpture or other crafted object, usually smaller and less detailed than the finished item.

Marbling A technique of decorating paper by floating colours on a liquid to form swirling patterns, often resembling those of marble. The pattern thus formed is then transferred to a sheet of paper. The easiest way to marble involves a combination of oil paint and water, which don't mix. A more complex technique involves floating watercolours on a gelatinous size made from caragheen moss (Irish seaweed).

Mitre Short for mitre joint: a corner joint, formed between two pieces of paper that are cut at 45° angles to make a perfect fit.

Oxidization The reaction of metal with oxygen, which causes tarnishing.

Paste A simple adhesive mixed from wheat flour and water. This is sold in numerous commercial variants, such as wallpaper (wheat) paste.

Plaster of Paris A white powder that sets to a hard solid when mixed with water.

Polyurethane A type of synthetic varnish.

Pyrography Controlled burning or blackening, using a woodburning tool.

Pulp A reduced paper and water mixture that, combined with a paste or glue, can be applied to an armature or mould or sculpted free-hand, like clay.

PVA (polyvinyl acetate) adhesive (white glue) A relatively quick-drying adhesive, which can also be used as a sealant.

Ragging A decorative technique whereby paint or glaze is removed in a mottled design using a cloth dampened with turpentine. Alternatively, paint may be added to create a similar effect.

Releasing agent A film placed over a mould to prevent the papier mâché from sticking to it – for example, a layer of petroleum jelly, or a sheet of clear plastic wrap/saran wrap.

Resist pattern A pattern made by masking parts of the paper with wax or some other material, then applying colour over the surface, leaving the masked areas unaffected.

Scumble An upper layer of paint added to modify the colour of the surface to which it is applied.

Size A weak paste on which marbling colours are floated, instead of on water, to give more control over the pattern. Also, size is used as a constituent of gesso.

Tempera A medium for powder paints, usually made from egg yolk and water.

Template A shape which can be used again and again as a basis for making a series of identical objects.

Water gilding A method of gilt decoration, less durable than oil gilding but with the advantage that it can be burnished.

Whiting A finely powdered chalk.

Woodburning tool A tool for controlled burning, rather like a soldering iron.

FOOTNOTES

1. J. T. Smith, *Nollekens and His Times*, Henry Colburn, London, 1828

2. Jo Elizabeth Gerken, *Wonderful Dolls of Papier Mâché,* Doll Research Associates, Nebraska, 1970

3. Yvonne Jones, *Georgian and Victorian Japanned Wares of the West Midlands,* Wolverhampton Art Gallery, England, 1982, p11

4. ibid, p10

5. F.P. and M.M. Verney, *Memoires of the Verney Family,* London, 1907

6. Edith R. Wyle, *Traditional Toys of Japan,* catalogue to an exhibition at the Craft and Folk Art Museum, Los Angeles, May 1st-June 25th 1979

7. Dona Z. Meilach, *Papier Mâché Artistry*, Allen and Unwin, London, Creative Craft Series, 1971

ARTISTS' ADDRESSES

The artists listed below
made and kindly loaned
the papier mâché pieces
that were photographed
for this book.

Brian Bishop
28 Grove Road East
Christchurch
Dorset BH23 2DQ

Norma Bottell
46 Park Road
Sittingbourne
Kent ME10 1DY

Kevin Brockbank
53 Updown Hill
Windlesham
Surrey GU20 6DW

Henny Burnett
18 Avenell Road
London N5 1DP

Mike Chase
c/o Gary Carter
12 Newick Road
Clapton
London E5

Madeleine Child
86 Alderney Street
London SW1

Priya Commander
Unit 7 Studios & Gallery
rear of 36/38 Peckham Road
Camberwell
London SE5

Philip Cox
12 Hartwood Drive
Stapleford
Nottingham
NG9 8HF

Jo Dixon
30 Southlain
Witney, Oxfordshire
OX8 7HZ

Theodora Fandousi
22 Walpole Street
Whitmore Reams
Wolverhampton
WV6 0AT

Caroline Gibbs
25 Henning Street
London SW11 3DR

Maureen Hamilton-Hill
56a King Henry's Road
London NW3 3RP

Jeff Higley
26 Homecroft Road
Siddenham
London SE26 5QG

Alison Lockhead
c/o Vicky Manning
9 Priory Terrace
Cheltenham
Gloucestershire
GLZ 6DS

Jane Macartney
Cassada Bay Hotel
Carriacou
Near Grenada
West Indies

Julia Manheim
A-Z Studios
5 Hardwidge Street
London SE1 3SY

Carey Mortimer
1 Kinloss Cottages
Kinloss Estate
Cupar
Fife KY15 4ND
Scotland

Jennie Neame
15 Stanley Buildings
Stanley Passage
Pancras Road
London NW1

Billy Nicholas
Kingsgate Workshops
110–116 Kingsgate Road
London NW6

Carolyn Quartermaine
72 Philbeech Gardens
London SW5

Keith Roberts
9a Wellfield Road
Roath
Cardiff CF2 3N2

Deborah Schneebeli-Morrell
10 York Rise
London NW5

Kate Sheppard
113 Slad Place
Stroud
Gloucestershire
GL5 1QZ

Sarah Simpson
42 Bovtown
Glastonbury
Somerset BA6 8JE

Malcolm Temple
36c Trebovir Road
London SW5

Yanina Temple
15 York Road
Loughborough
Leicestershire LE11 3DA

Louise Vergette
59 Quantock Road
Windmill Hill
Bristol BS3 4PQ

Katherine Virgils
43 Cambridge Gardens
London W10

Melinda While
18 Glenshaw Mansions
South Island Place
Brixton Road
London SW9 0DS

Melanie Williams
Bronllys Castle
Bronllys
Brecon, Powys
LD3 0HL

*Page 139: Yanina
Temple (top),
Kate Sheppard (bottom)*

*Right: Parakeet Singh
(Katherine Virgils)*

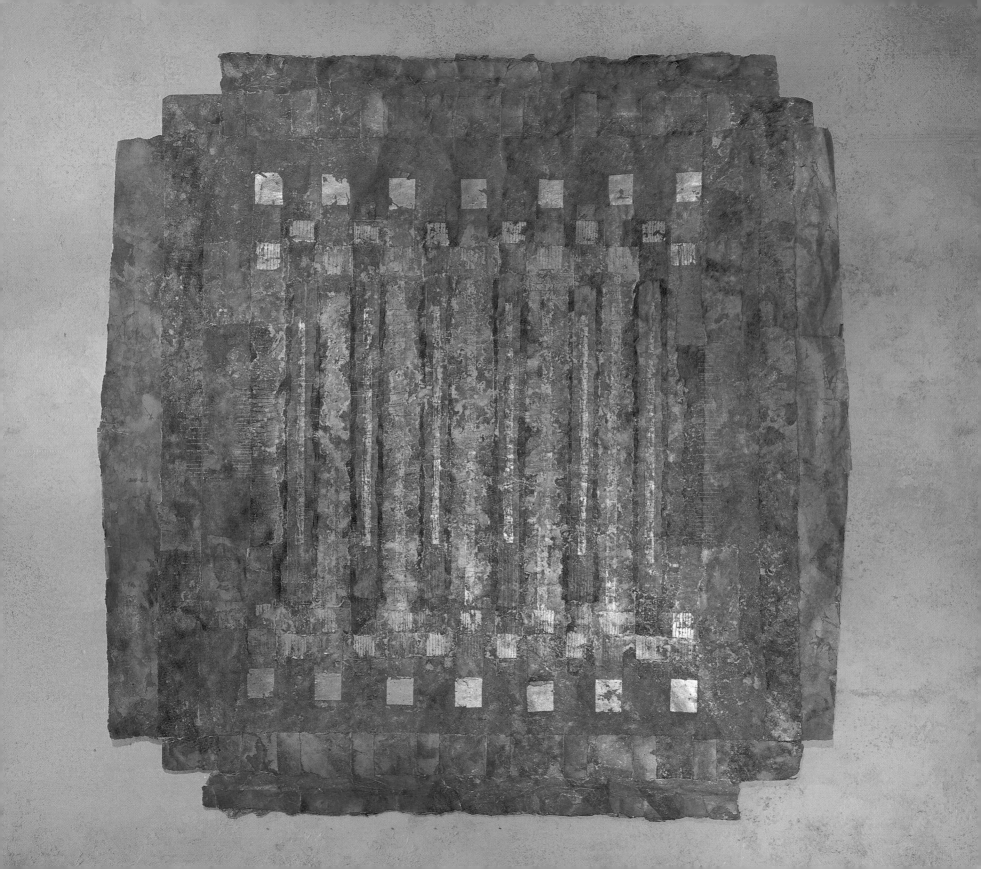

INDEX

Main entries are in **bold**.
Page numbers in *italics* refer to step-by-step instructions.